Economic Development

ECONOMICS TODAY
Edited by Andrew Leake

The 'Economics Today' series surveys contemporary headline topics in applied economics. Each book in the series is written by an expert in the field in a style that is fluently readable. It serves the student of introductory economic principles while also making the subject accessible to a more general reader. The series embraces the problem-solving skills of the new generation of students and stresses the importance of real-world issues and the significance of economic ideas.

Published:

Jean-Louis Barsoux and Peter Lawrence:
  The Challenge of British Management
Andy Beharrell: **Unemployment and Job Creation**
S. F. Goodman: **The European Union** (3rd edition)
Nigel Healey and Mark Cook: **Growth and Structural Change**
Ian Hodge: **Environmental Choices**
Andrew Leake: **The Economic Question**
Kent Matthews: **Macroeconomics and the Market**
Gareth Rees and Charles Smith: **Economic Development** (2nd edition)
Jenny Wales: **Investigating Social Issues**
John Wigley and Carol Lipman: **The Enterprise Economy**
Margaret Wilkinson: **Taxation**

Series Standing Order

If you would like to receive future titles in this series as they are published, you can make use of our standing order facility. To place a standing order please contact your bookseller or, in case of difficulty, write to us at the address below with your name and address and the name of the series. Please state with which title you wish to begin your standing order. (If you live outside the United Kingdom we may not have the rights for your area, in which case we will forward your order to the publisher concerned.)

Customer Services Department, Macmillan Distribution Ltd
Houndmills, Basingstoke, Hampshire RG21 2XS, England

ECONOMIC DEVELOPMENT

Second Edition

Gareth Rees and Charles Smith

palgrave

First edition 1994
Reprinted three times
Second edition 1998

Published by
PALGRAVE
Houndmills, Basingstoke, Hampshire RG21 6XS and
175 Fifth Avenue, New York, N. Y. 10010
Companies and representatives throughout the world

PALGRAVE is the new global academic imprint of
St. Martin's Press LLC Scholarly and Reference Division and
Palgrave Publishers Ltd (formerly Macmillan Press Ltd).

ISBN 0–333–72228–0

This book is printed on paper suitable for recycling and
made from fully managed and sustained forest sources.

A catalogue record for this book is available
from the British Library.

10   9
08   07   06   05   04

Printed and bound in Great Britain by
Antony Rowe Limited, Chippenham, Wiltshire

Dedications:

Irene Rees, my mother

D. G. R.

* * *

Francis Archie Smith, Mary Louise Quibell, José Brocca
Ramón, and Rosa García López; my grandparents,
mis abuelos

C. E. S.

Make John Lennon's dream come true . . .
It's the least we can do.

Song by Gerry Murray (Brandon Publishers), performed by Christy Moore (WEA Records).

Contents

List of Tables, Figures and Boxes

Tables

Figures

Boxes

Acknowledgements

The authors and publishers wish to thank the following copyright holders and sources of statistical information for permission to reproduce copyright material:

Bank of England, Organisation for Economic Cooperation and Development, Oxfam, Oxford University Press, United Nations Development Programme, United Nations Children's Fund, World Bank, World Health Organisation, *Finance and Development*, *New Internationalist*.

Every effort has been made to contact copyright holders for permission to reproduce material in this book, but if any have been inadvertently overlooked, the publishers would be pleased to make the necessary arrangement at the earliest opportunity.

Ian Dorton (Sevenoaks School) and Deon Glover (Atlantic College) kindly allowed the use of diagrams developed in their teaching. Oscar Asumang (Hermann Gmeiner College, Ghana) provided useful comments on the first edition. We are also grateful for feedback from students at Swansea Institute of Higher Education and the United World College of the Atlantic; and for constructive criticism from teachers we have met at workshops and conferences around the world.

Like all textbook authors, we have to apologise to our families for neglecting them while writing, so special thanks are due to: Ellie, Tom and William Rees; and Julia, Sally and Matthew Smith.

Finally we wish to record our thanks to Andrew Leake, Steven Rutt, Nicola Young, Sarah Brown, Gwen Allingham and the entire publishing team for their continuing long-term commitment to this book.

All errors and omissions are our own responsibility.

D. G. R.
C. E. S.

Preface to the First Edition

Development Economics has a reputation for being a particularly difficult branch of an already difficult subject. This is partly due to the fact that textbooks on development tend to be either encyclopaedic works for degree students, or in-depth studies of narrow topics aimed at the high-level specialist. In contrast, this book is meant to be an 'entry-level' text, suitable for economics candidates at A-Level (where development is likely to increase in importance as syllabuses adopt an 'issues based' approach); and also suitable for equivalent examinations such as the International Baccalaureate (where development is already an important part of the curriculum). Additionally, it should be useful to students of related subjects, such as geography; to undergraduates embarking on a study of development; and to the general reader.

It is therefore hoped that this little book will have something of value for young economists who wish to be shown ways in which their chosen subject is of vital importance in the real world; for teachers who wish to give higher priority to development topics; and for readers of all ages who wish to take an informed interest in these important issues.

In a book of this size it is not possible to address all development issues in detail, and so some selection has taken place. An attempt has been made to address those aspects of development which relate to the themes of 'growth' and 'welfare'; and to discuss issues which give the student of introductory economics a chance to see some applications of basic economic theory, and to use the language of economics in a development context.

Readers wishing to continue their interest in development with further reading can safely afford to avoid most of the British tabloid press, where foreign news reporting tends to range in standard from non-existent to appallingly xenophobic. It is no wonder that so many readers of most examples of this genre appear to have difficulty in regarding themselves as Europeans, let alone as world citizens. Of the broadsheet papers, the *Financial Times* can be singled out for its regular in-depth surveys of particular countries, and *The Independent*, *The Observer* and *The European* often focus on particular development issues. The 'EG' supplement of the education section of *The Guardian* very often contains a great deal of useful information, of interest to both teachers and students. Probably the most efficient way of keeping in touch with development issues is to follow the themes presented every week in *The Economist* and in the monthly *New Internationalist*, and I think that it is fair to say that these journals view matters from rather different political stances.

Somewhat in advance of anticipated changes in the A-Level economics syllabuses, the editors of *The Economic Review* and *Economics and Business Education* (formerly *Economics*) show commendable willingness to carry articles covering development topics. It is to be hoped that this healthy trend will continue, and that students will be encouraged to follow the new opportunities to study development economics which should become available in the near future.

Among official publications I would strongly recommend the World Bank's *World Development Report* and the United Nations Development Programme's *Human Development Report*, whose findings feature strongly in parts of this book. These are annual publications, and something which makes them particularly interesting is the way in which they usually deal with a particular theme each year.

On BBC Radio 4, programmes such as *Analysis* and *From Our Own Correspondent* sometimes touch on development issues. While there are occasional emotional appeals at the time of some obvious disaster, mainstream television largely ignores the less developed countries. The so-called 'minority' channels are honourable exceptions. It is particularly worth seeking out relevant Open University programmes on BBC2, and any repeats of the excellent *One World* series screened on Channel 4 during the 1992 Rio Summit Conference on the Environment.

As mentioned earlier, a book of limited size and scope has to be selective in its approach. During the important gestation period, I found the aforementioned sources of great value in helping me to select some themes and issues as being particularly worth highlighting in this book.

I hope that students using this book will find themselves just a little better equipped to follow development issues, wherever they are discussed, with a critical awareness.

C. E. S.

Preface to the Second Edition

The first edition of this book was something of a speculative venture, written in anticipation of major changes in economics syllabuses. While the book has established itself as an important resource for entry-level courses in the field, economic development has become a popular and significant part of pre-university courses, notably the A-Level syllabuses offered by the Cambridge and London boards; and university students have continued to show a growing interest in a systematic study of development issues. Meanwhile, the International Baccalaureate has undergone an exciting curriculum review which has confirmed the central role of development economics as part of the education of its world-wide clientele. This has happened against a background of growing concern in the media and among political and business circles for themes such as 'globalisation' and principles such as 'polluter pays' which are germane to development.

This second edition therefore demonstrates enough confidence in the role of an entry-level text of this kind to enable us to shorten its title to *Economic Development* (from *Economic Development, Growth and Welfare*). Since economic development can now be regarded as a mainstream subject area, there is no need to hedge our bets to widen the audience, although 'growth' and 'welfare' are still important themes within the book. The new edition also benefits from the input of a second author who has unrivalled experience of teaching development issues at this level.

The opportunity has been taken to correct some minor errors from the first edition, to up-date information sources (particularly in the later chapters whose 'macro' nature is more prone to built-in obsolescence), and to expand some sections in the light of recent developments. We therefore hope to have improved on and supplemented rather than replaced a successful framework which has been well received by teachers, lecturers, examiners and students.

We should also mention that Macmillan's academic and professional catalogue contains a large number of books at university level on development topics.

Gareth Rees, St Donats;
Charles Smith, Bridgend;
Wales.

List of Abbreviations

ASEAN	Association of South East Asian Nations
CAFOD	Catholic Fund for Overseas Development
CAP	Common Agricultural Policy
DAC	Development Assistance Committee
EBRD	European Bank for Reconstruction and Development
EFTA	European Free Trade Association
ERM	Exchange Rate Mechanism
EU	European Union
FAO	Food and Agriculture Organisation
FDI	foreign direct investment
FTA	free trade area
GATT	General Agreement on Tariffs and Trade
GDP	gross domestic product
GNNP	green net national product
GNP	gross national product
HDI	Human Development Index
HDR	Human Development Report
HPI	Human Poverty Index
HYV	high-yielding varieties (of cereal)
IBRD	International Bank for Reconstruction and Development
IDA	International Development Association
IFAD	International Fund for Agricultural Development
IFC	International Finance Corporation

IMF	International Monetary Fund
IPPF	International Planned Parent Federation
ITC	International Tin Council
LDCs	less developed countries
LRAC	long run average cost curve
MAI	Multilateral Agreement on Investment
MDCs	more developed countries
MEW	measure of economic welfare
MFA	Multi-fibre Agreement
MFN	most favoured nation
MIGA	Multilateral Investment Guarantee Agency
MNE	multinational enterprise
MRP	marginal revenue product
MTN	multinational trade negotiations
NAFTA	North American Free Trade Area
NGO	non-governmental organisation
NIC	newly industrialised countries
NSP	net social product
ODA	official development assistance
OECD	Organisation for Economic Cooperation and Development
OPEC	Organisation of Petroleum Exporting Countries
OXFAM	Oxford Committee for Famine Relief
PPC	production possibility curve
PPP	purchasing power parity
R&D	research and development
SDR	Special Drawing Rights
TRIMS	trade related investment measures
TRIPS	trade related intellectual property rights
UNCTAD	United Nations Conference on Trade and Development
UNDP	United Nations Development Programme
UNICEF	United Nations Childrens Fund
VER	voluntary export restraint
WDR	World Development Report
WHO	World Health Organisation
WIPO	World Intellectual Property Organisation
WTO	World Trade Organisation

The World and its Welfare

1

Economists are notorious for using three long words where one short one will do. This is one reason why the subject of economics, which in fact revolves around a handful of essentially simple concepts, has gained an undeserved reputation among its students for being horrendously difficult.

Economic development is a branch of economics which has attracted more than its fair share of pieces of jargon, some of which have become inappropriate. It no longer makes sense to talk of the 'First World' of richer countries and 'Third World' of poorer countries, when the 'Second World' of planned economies is no longer a recognisable group. The artificial division into 'North' and 'South' with the implication that North equals 'rich' while South equals 'poor' is neither accurate nor helpful (Japan is south of Bosnia). If we refer to some countries as 'developed', does this not betray our feeling that they have achieved something superior to being 'not developed'? And furthermore, is it not possible for a 'developed' country to either develop further still or, indeed, to 'de-develop' in some way? What is a *developing country*, and how does it differ from a *newly industrialised country* (NIC)? What do we mean when we say that a country is 'rich'? What do we mean by 'poor'? In what ways can a country be 'backward'?

The problem with many of these words and phrases is that they rest upon unstated assumptions and value judgements. For example, if we refer to some countries as 'underdeveloped' it suggests that in an ideal world, all countries would be fully developed, manufacturing exporters. Is this possible? Is it desirable when there is a strong body of opinion among environmentalists that some countries are 'over-developed'? If we refer to poorer countries as 'developing countries', then this might betray an underlying feeling that developing is what they *ought* to be doing; or it might simply be an inaccurate description, because developing might be something which they are manifestly not doing.

In this book two acronyms are used quite often: MDC to refer to a 'more developed country'; LDC to refer to a 'less developed country'. Other terms, such as 'newly industrialised country', 'Third World', or 'North and South', are used only where they provide a useful extra category for the discussion in hand, or where they are used in quotations or as part of data imported from other sources.

Describing countries as 'more developed' or 'less developed' enables us, in principle, to refer to them in a non-prejudicial way provided that we can form a clear picture of what we mean by 'development' (as attempted in Chapter 2) and is a useful and workable convention.

Those staid purists who deny that their economics is 'normative' are likely to have an unhappy time in the field of economic development, because here we cannot be 'value-free'. Many would say that we *ought* not to be value-free (itself a normative statement). Economics is about 'What? How? and For Whom?' Development economics is especially about 'For Whom?' and this is only superficially a technical question which can be reduced to sets of graphs and formulae. Ultimately, deep down, it is a moral question, to do with 'justice' and 'fairness'. Generally, however, economists are not terribly good at discussing questions of fairness. They prefer to try to deal with what can be measured.

Income, Growth and Welfare

How can we measure *income*? What do we mean by *growth*? Is a growth in income necessarily the same thing as an increase in *living standards*? Are living standards the same thing as *welfare*?

National income

National income can be defined as the total value of factor incomes in one country in one year. However, economists recognise that national income is created by the output of goods and services, and by expenditure on those goods and services. One person's expenditure is another person's income, and yet another person's output. Thus, if you purchase a new bicycle, this represents expenditure to you, but income to the seller; it also represents a quantity of output from the bicycle industry. Statisticians who calculate national income figures therefore use three methods:

1. the *expenditure* method, which calculates the total amount of spending on goods and services;
2. the *output* method, which estimates the total value of goods and services produced;
3. the *income* method, which measures the total amount of incomes earned.

Economists and statisticians have developed the collection of national income accounts into a fine art; indeed, the comprehensiveness and reliability of a government's national income statistics could perhaps be regarded as one test of the 'economic development' of the country in question. The published figures have two broad uses. Firstly, they can be used to help to chart the economic progress of a single country over time; secondly they can be used to help compare the progress of different countries. In short, they can be used for *single-country* comparisons and *international* comparisons.

A study of the *National Income Blue Book* of the UK government, for example, reveals a wealth of economic data. There is information on spending patterns, earnings, investment, the balance of payments, and much more. Comparing such data with publications from, say, the Indian government would reveal many insights into the different nature of the two economies. In order to assist in such comparisons, economists have attempted over a number of years to standardise the methods of calculation and terminology used in the accounts. In theory, all three methods of calculation should give an identical total; in practice, a number of adjustments have to be made to bring them into equality. Reference can be made to any standard A-Level economics textbook for a full description of these adjustments. Here, we will confine ourselves to a discussion of some concepts which are crucial to our discussion.

National income is known in technical terms as *net national product at factor cost*. Within this phrase, the word 'product' draws attention to the fact that income is not a purely 'monetary' phenomenon; in other words, creating money does not necessarily create income. What does create income is the output of something *real*: the production of goods and services. The term 'factor cost' indicates that the value of the output is related to the cost of the factors used in production. This is not necessarily the same thing as national product at 'market prices' since market prices can be increased above the level of their true factor cost by indirect taxes, or reduced by subsidies. The word 'net' indicates that depreciation or capital consumption has been allowed for. This is necessary because in the production of anything, there is some 'wear and tear' on producer goods, and some national expenditure therefore has to be devoted to the replacement of worn out plant, machinery, and other items. Thus, net national product is invariably a lower figure than *gross national product (GNP) at factor cost*, which includes expenditure on all types of investment goods, whether or not this investment is in additional capacity, or merely replaces old items.

The word 'national' indicates that the figure includes *net property income from abroad*. This is income earned by assets situated in other countries, owned by domestic residents, less income earned by assets located in the domestic economy paid to foreigners abroad. These flows of interest and profits arise from international investment. If, for example, a UK resident owns shares in a German chemical company, then the German plant contributes to German national income through providing output, income and employment in Germany; but it also contributes to the UK national income when dividends are paid to the British shareholder. Subtracting net property income from gross national product at factor cost gives a total known as *gross domestic product (GDP) at factor cost*; this is a measure of the total value of goods and services produced in a year within the geographical boundaries of a country.

Domestic or national?

GDP is measured regardless of whether the income generated by domestic output is received by domestic citizens or foreigners abroad.

As far as the USA, Japan, and the economies of Western Europe are concerned, there is usually only a small difference between GDP and GNP, with GDP being slightly smaller. However, there are circumstances in which the difference can be quite large.

In countries like Thailand, Malaysia, Chile, and South Africa, where many assets are owned by foreign companies, GNP can be some 15 per cent smaller than GDP. GNP is also lowered in countries suffering from the 'Third World Debt' problem which have to pay interest on borrowings from institutions abroad. However, most international investment occurs because multinational companies in one MDC invest in assets in another MDC; this causes flows of income between MDCs themselves rather than between MDCs and LDCs. In spite of the debt-servicing problems of many LDCs, GNP is slightly higher than GDP for LDCs as a whole. Two factors which contribute to this are the returns on investments made in the west in the 1970s and 1980s by the oil exporting countries; and the growing tendency for migrant workers from the LDCs to seek employment in the MDCs and send part of their earnings back to families still living in their home countries.

In measuring economic growth the index which is generally used is GNP per capita (per head), although United States economists often prefer to use GDP per head. Whether either is an adequate way of measuring 'development' or whether the 'quality of life' of a population has improved is a topic to which we will return.

What is Economic Growth?

Economic growth takes place when there is either an increase in the national income of a country, or in the country's productive capacity, (this productive capacity being a country's ability to generate national income). Economists have a theoretical tool known as a *production possibility curve* (PPC) which can be used to analyse these concepts of growth.

Figure 1.1 shows all the possible combinations of two goods which can be produced at any one time, given existing resources. If all resources are devoted to producing Good X, then ON units can be produced. If, however, all resources are used to produce Good Y, then OM units can be produced. If a combination of X and Y is desired, then all possible combinations are shown by the line MN which is

FIGURE 1.1
A Production Possibility Curve

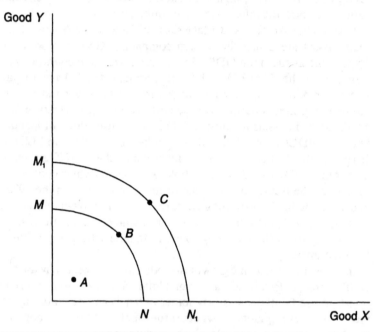

drawn convex to the the origin. This line shows both *factor combination* and *factor substitution*. It shows how a country's factors of production can be combined in different ways in order to vary the pattern of output. It also shows how factors can be substituted for each other in order to produce less of one good and more of another. For example, suppose Good Y represents 'tanks' and Good X represents 'tractors'. The PPC can now be used to give some interesting insights into the 'peace dividend' resulting from the end of the Cold War and the switching of war industries into peaceful uses. Producing half as many tanks will not necessarily double the amount of tractors. In the language of economics, we can say that this is because the factors of production are not 'perfectly mobile', or that one factor is not a 'perfect substitute' for another. In other words, tank factories, machines designed for tank production, and people trained to build tanks, cannot be instantly switched to tractor production: factories will need re-organising, machines will need re-designing, modification or even re-building, and workers will need to be re-trained. Thus the law of 'diminishing returns' operates as factors are switched from one use to another, and the output of tractors rises less than proportionately to the falling output of tanks.

The PPC represents a 'frontier' or 'boundary' in the sense that given the current availability of resources and technical knowledge, a country cannot produce on a point to the right of the PPC. The PPC is therefore a 'short run' diagram: in the long run the productive capacity of a country can be increased, thus shifting the PPC to the right. It is often assumed that the natural tendency is for the PPC of any country to shift in this way, but there are circumstances when it could shift to the left, where a country is laid waste by warfare, disease or natural disasters, for instance.

The PPC can also be used to to examine the output of more than two goods. The vertical axis could, for instance, represent 'all capital goods' and the horizontal axis could represent 'all consumption goods'. The PPC then becomes a useful tool for examining the opportunity cost of investment; that is, the sacrifice necessary for a country's citizens to be willing to invest. A greater expenditure on capital goods involves the sacrifice of present consumption, and depends on people being willing to wait for consumption goods. The extent to which people are willing to make this sacrifice depends on what sociologists call 'deferred gratification patterns' or what economists call people's 'time preferences'. Do people prefer consumption immediately, or would they prefer consumption at a higher level tomorrow? Some bars of chocolate now, or more bars of chocolate in the future? If the promise of 'chocolate tomorrow' is convincing enough, then people might be willing to invest in chocolate-making machinery now in order to enjoy a higher rate of consumption later. It could be argued that this is what has enabled planned economies such as the former Soviet Union to industrialise so rapidly in the twentieth century. Power stations, railways, hospitals and nuclear weapons were built at the expense of chocolate bars, denim jeans, hamburgers and conditioning shampoo. It could further be argued that the recent move towards a market economy results partly from the strain of the central planners attempting to impose time preferences which were not always shared by the mass of the population.

A country which chooses a higher level of investment in the short run can expect, if the new capital is effective and productive, to experience a more rapid shift of the PPC than a country which prefers immediate consumption. This leads us to one definition of economic growth, which is sometimes referred to as the process of increasing the productive capacity of a country. This type of growth would be shown by a rightward shift of the PPC, and is sometimes called *potential* growth.

Potential growth is the rate at which a country's economy could grow, if all its resources (workers, machines, factories, etc.) were fully employed. Potential economic growth can be increased by such methods as increasing or discovering new resources: by increasing population, or mining for newly discovered minerals, for instance. It can also be increased by improving the *productivity* of existing resources: by training workers, inventing new technology, improving organisation, or adopting better production methods.

Potential growth can be distinguished from *actual* growth. This is the annual rate of change of national output; that is, the growth of goods and services actually produced. This depends on the degree of utilisation of productive capacity. If there are empty factories and/or unemployed people in a country, then these are signs that there are unemployed resources. A movement from point A to point B on the PPC diagram would represent actual economic growth; a shift of the PPC to M_1N_1 would represent potential growth, but would not represent actual growth unless the combination of goods being produced moved from B to C. Statistics referring to growth rates refer to actual growth; when statistics are produced showing a recession or unemployment, then these indicate a gap between actual and potential growth. If growth in the short run is to be sustained in the long run, then both actual and potential growth are necessary.

Actual growth tends to fluctuate in a cyclical fashion. Market economies go through periodic phases of 'boom' and 'recession', often referred to as the *trade cycle* (or *business cycle*). Keynesian economists stress the importance of short-run influences on aggregate demand and suggest ways in which governments can attempt to achieve steady actual growth while also attempting to achieve other macroeconomic objectives such as full employment, stable prices and equilibrium in the balance of payments. These are known as 'demand management' policies.

The growth of potential output tends to be less cyclical and more stable, and it is this type of growth which is specially relevant to development economics. Attempts to achieve potential growth focus less on demand management and more on the 'supply side' of the economy. In some of the MDCs the term 'supply side' has to some extent been hijacked by economists with a rather narrow, (some would say 'right wing') agenda for reducing 'market imperfections' and increasing 'labour flexibility'. This is a pity, because all economists, but especially those concerned with economic development, need to be concerned about measures which can be used to increase a country's productive capacity.

GNP and Living Standards

Suppose 'Karenia' has twice the GNP of its neighbouring country, 'Alisonia'. Does this necessarily mean that the average citizen of Karenia has twice the 'standard of living' of a counterpart in Alisonia? We can answer this question with a resounding and definite 'maybe'.

The concept of *standard of living* is a vague one, and there is no widely accepted and watertight definition; however it is linked to the ability of people to purchase goods and services. To have a command over goods and services people need income, and since GNP is generated by income, output and expenditure, it is *likely* that citizens of a country with a growing GNP will experience an increase in living standards, and it is also likely that people in a country with a high level of GNP will enjoy a higher standard of living than those in a country with a lower GNP. Certainly, in the MDCs, economic growth is something which is taken for granted, and any government which fails to deliver a year-by-year increase in GNP finds that this is noticed by enough citizens to make it dread the results of the next round of elections. Higher incomes and higher levels of consumption have come to be expected, and they are seen to be linked to growth of GNP. Linked, but not equal to, however, and as a set of statistics GNP levels and growth rates must be treated with some caution, as they are not a perfect indicator of living standards. There are several reasons for this.

First we must assume that the authorities of Karenia and Alisonia use statistical methods which are similar, and that their collection of statistics is equally accurate. In practice, this might not be the case. One country might for instance, have a large *parallel economy* where transactions take place without official records being kept. This might be done for illicit reasons, such as the avoidance of tax; or it might be done quite innocently. In Alisonia, for example, climate, soil and land ownership might be such that people are able to grow a substantial proportion of their own food; whereas in Karenia people are more likely to purchase foodstuffs from shops. This would register as a higher level of GNP for Karenia, without necessarily implying a higher standard of living. Economists can overcome such problems to some extent, by estimating *imputed* values. This is done, for instance, in the case of owner-occupied housing. If in Karenia most people rent houses, whereas in Alisonia most people are owner-occupiers, this would increase the measured GNP of Karenia relative to Alisonia. Economists overcome this problem by calculating an 'imputed' rent, i.e. by assuming that owner-occupiers can be considered to be their own landlords, paying themselves rent for living in their own houses.

It could be argued that there are other activities to which an imputed value could be attached. If, for instance, every family in Alisonia stopped doing their own (unpaid) housework, but instead sent a family member to work a set number of hours a day as a housekeeper for their neighbour at an hourly rate of pay, no family would be any better or worse off financially as each one would receive the same wage as they paid out. But the measured national income of Alisonia would increase overnight. In making international comparisons, what is important is that statisticians and economists should use similar techniques and methods; so either no countries would need to make an allowance for imputed housework payments, or they all should.

It is also possible that the statisticians in each country use different formulae for calculating such things as trade balances and retail price indexes. We might also have the problem of converting the statistics of one country into the currency of another.

Even if these practical problems are overcome, then there is a very obvious reason why a GNP figure twice that of another country's does not necessarily imply a higher living standard. Karenia, for example, might have twice the GNP of Alisonia, but also twice the population to clothe, house, feed, educate, and so on. This problem is overcome by dividing GNP by the size of the population to give a *per capita* figure. Even this has its complications, because it says nothing about the *composition* of the population: its age structure for instance. Different age groups have different economic needs. If the people of

Alisonia are largely of working age, while Karenia consists of a large number of infants and very old people, then this could well reduce the average living standard in Karenia as a larger proportion of the country's resources will need to be diverted to meeting the needs of its dependants.

Similarly, merely dividing GNP by the size of the population gives us an average figure which tells us nothing about the *distribution* of income. If Karenia's GNP per head is £10 000, this does not necessarily mean that every man, woman and child has access to £10000 of spending power each year. It could be that Karenia has income concentrated in the hands of a few people, while Alisonia has a larger 'middle class'. The figure of £10 000 per year is also a *flow* concept, which means that it is measured over time, and shows how much income is received each year. It does not tell us about the *stock* concept of accumulated past incomes, or *wealth*; and if people in Alisonia have a larger amount of inherited land, buildings and other assets than those in Karenia, they might be able to enjoy a higher standard of living even if their annual monetary income is smaller.

A higher GNP per capita for Karenia compared with Alisonia does not necessarily indicate a higher standard of living if the *cost* of living is higher in Karenia. Similarly, an increase in the GNP per capita of Karenia does not necessarily indicate an increase in living standards if Karenia experiences inflation. Economists therefore distinguish between *nominal income* (GNP at current prices) and *real income* (GNP at constant prices).

In order to compare 'like with like' it is necessary to have some idea of the level of personal disposable income in each country: that is, income after taxes have been deducted. Also, it is necessary to be aware of the 'social wage' received by the citizens of each country, that is, to estimate a value of any services provided free at the point of need and paid for through general taxation: such items as health, education, pensions and unemployment benefit. If such things are received as of right in Alisonia, but have to be paid for out of disposable income in Karenia, then this might give a totally different perspective on living standards than GNP per capita.

Lastly, we need to look at the composition of national expenditure, not just at its total value. For example, Karenia might be a cold country where citizens have to devote a larger share of their income to clothing, heating and fuel bills; the citizens of Alisonia might benefit from a milder climate and thus have more choice as to how to spend their income. Karenia might be at war; its high level of national output might be largely expended on bullets and missiles which literally go up in smoke, whereas Alisonia's apparently lower GNP per head is devoted to peaceful uses which directly benefit its citizens.

Living Standards and Welfare

In order to understand the concept of economic welfare it is first necessary to understand the idea of an *externality*.

In the production or consumption of any good or service there are costs and benefits. Many of these are *internal* or *private* costs which means that they are fully paid or received by the producer or consumer in question. For example, purchasing a new car creates a private cost for the consumer, represented by the price paid to the car dealer. Production and consumption also results in external costs and benefits, which are not paid or received by the producer or consumer, but instead 'spill over' into the community at large. Thus a negative externality resulting from the use of a car is created by the pollution emanating from the exhaust pipe. An external cost is sometimes termed a *negative externality*, while an external benefit is known as a *positive externality*. Internal costs plus external costs give a total which is known as *social costs*; internal benefits plus external benefits equal *social benefits*. If social costs are subtracted from social benefits then the result is known as *net social product* (NSP). If Karenia suffers from a high level of pollution; if long working hours cause marital problems and stress; if, in turn, a lot of working hours are lost through stress-related diseases; if it has a high suicide rate; if crime rates are high; then a high GNP per head might contribute to the welfare of its citizens less than a negative net social product subtracts from it.

Measuring some external costs and benefits can be very difficult in practice. Some people would argue that if an acceptable method of quantifying them were to become widely accepted, there would still be some way to go to fully measure welfare. This is because account should be made of certain items which are in essence unquantifiable: such things as the stability of the social and political climate; a country's atmosphere of law and order, and people's tastes. The populations of some countries might be happier with a relatively low level of consumption if it means freedom from some of the stresses and strains of a consumer society. We should not assume that money can buy happiness: perhaps the best that can be said of it is that it does help to take people's minds off unhappiness!

The American economists Nordhaus and Tobin have developed what they call a *measure of economic welfare* (MEW). This starts with GNP and adds to it an allowance for leisure, non-marketed goods and services (such as housework) and public amenities such as roads. Some items are then subtracted. Nordhaus and Tobin describe some of these items as 'bads' or 'disamenities, such as pollution, and others as 'regrettables', such as expenditure on defence and travelling time spent commuting to work. They argue that generally MEW grows at a slower pace than GNP. This is because leisure and non-marketed activities have been growing at a slower rate than the output of goods and services, while the output of bads and regrettables has been growing faster.

An attempt to quantify the unquantifiable has important repercussions for economic development, as it gives us some indications of the role of governments in the development process. Economic welfare is likely to be increased if negative NSPs are taxed, while positive NSPs are subsidised.

Development:
Economic and
Human

2

What is development? Is it the same thing as growth? In this chapter we will discuss two concepts: economic development and human development.

Growth and Development

In the previous chapter we distinguished between actual and potential growth.

The word 'development' signifies changes which are permanent. It is true that actual growth can sometimes lead to a 'ratchet' effect, where a country permanently achieves a higher level of welfare than it had previously. However, it is quite possible for actual growth to be short lived: during a war, for example, a country might achieve remarkably high growth rates; but the physical output is immediately turned to dust as bombs and missiles are exploded, and at the end of this growth period the country as a whole could well be worse off than before.

The word 'development' implies that growth in one sector has substantial effects on other sectors as well. As far as potential growth is concerned however, a country's productive capacity might be expanded by growth in just a single sector: an oil producing country which expands its oil-related industries and discovers new reserves will experience potential growth.

Growth, whether actual or potential, is a concept which centres on 'quantity', whereas *development* also considers 'quality'. Growth takes place when there is an increase in the the per capita income or output of a country; development occurs when the costs of growth are minimised, and when the benefits of growth are distributed among the whole population. Development cannot be said to have taken place unless there have been improvements in the quality of life; improvements such as better living conditions, health care, improved diets, increased literacy and lower infant mortality rates. Cultural, recreational, and social amenities are also widely regarded as essential components of the quality of life.

Many development economists would today agree that in the past too much attention has been paid to economic growth, and not enough attention has been paid to the *reasons* for encouraging development: reducing poverty, increasing life expectancy, improving health, allowing people the freedom to take part in decision making, feeding the people. The Indian economist Amartya Sen, for example, has argued that starvation arises out of a lack of income with which to buy food, rather than a lack of availability of food, and that raising the incomes of the poor is the most efficient way of reducing undernourishment. Sen refers to development as the 'expansion of people's capabilities', and has encouraged economists to broaden their view of development, to include *value judgements* about what ought to be (i.e. *normative economics* as well as *positive economics*) and to argue that development policies should be 'capabilities-orientated' as well as 'goods-orientated'.

It is time to bring together some of the points made so far to form a working definition of development. We will consider two views of development; they are not incompatible with each other, but one is broader than the other, and we shall refer to them as economic development and human development.

Economic Development

Economic development can be regarded as a process of growth and change aimed at raising people's living standards. It involves growth in total and per capita income; and is accompanied by fundamental changes in the structure of an economy.

This corresponds closely to the view of development adopted by the World Bank, and whose progress is charted each year in the annual *World Development Report* (WDR), which puts nations in a rank order according mainly to their economic success. The rank order is essentially based on GNP per head, and its rate of change. Within this rank order it is possible to place a fairly arbitrary dividing line between countries which can be regarded as MDCs and those which are LDCs; and economists following the World Bank view would generally accept that this line occurs at a level of about $5000 of GNP per capita.

What is Human Development?

It would be possible to adopt the above definition of economic development, and conclude that 'development' can take place within a context of, say, racial discrimination, or in a country terrorised by a violent dictatorship. This could hardly be described as a satisfactory conclusion.

In 1990, the United Nations Development Programme (UNDP) launched a new *Human Development Index* (HDI) which is published each year in the *Human Development Report* (HDR) with information for each of 160 countries.

The UNDP defines human development as a 'process of enlarging people's choices'. Three choices are deemed to be critical: access to resources (purchasing power, which is calculated from GNP per capita and a calculation of the cost of living); a long and healthy life (as reflected by figures for life expectancy); and education (measured by the adult literacy rate). Figures are available for each of these, and they are combined to give a number which varies between 0 and 1: the closer to 1, the higher the level of human development.

The UNDP intends to refine the way in which it calculates the HDI in the years ahead. The authors of the HDR already compile figures relating to enrolment in tertiary education, infant mortality, the annual growth rate of the population, the percentage of the labour force in industry, the annual rate of inflation, savings as a percentage of GDP, trade dependency (exports plus imports as a percentage of GDP), the annual growth rate of GDP per capita, and the distribution of income; but as yet these indicators have not been incorporated into the HDI itself, nor have any of the various ratios that are sometimes used to indicate living standards, such as television sets per household, the percentage of households without bathrooms, doctors per head of population, soldiers per teacher, and so on. An even more ambitious aim is the intention to find ways of quantifying other social achievements that the UNDP sees as important for the quality of life: such things as political freedom and human rights.

The 1992 HDR put Canada at the top of the main HDI league table, replacing Japan (see Table 2.1). The UK was described as 'one of the world's best places to live – especially for men'. Interestingly, Germany was well ahead of the UK in terms of GNP per capita, but slightly behind in terms of the HDI. All but 6 of the last 35 countries were in Africa. The report drew attention to the fact that the fast-growing economies of South East Asia distorted the 'southern picture'. In the past decade there has been negative growth in Latin America, the Caribbean and sub-Saharan Africa. These areas, together with South Asia, have also suffered a decrease in their share of world trade. Capital has been gravitating towards the industrial countries where profit rates are higher, and real interest rates have been up to four times higher for poor nations than for rich ones. The UNDP concluded that a 'global compact' is necessary to redress the balance, and offered a 'visionary blueprint', including new institutions such as a Development Security Council at the UN, a global central bank with, in time, a common world currency, and a system of progressive income tax, to be collected automatically from the richer nations and distributed to the poorer ones according to their income and development needs.

While such solutions are a very, very long way away, the strength of the HDI is that it provides some evidence upon which policy makers can be urged to act. Hopefully, a greater awareness of global problems will promote a more internationalist outlook. In the area of migration, for example, the prospect of large movements of job-seeking people might encourage more aid from the MDCs to create employment in the LDCs; but on the other hand it is also encouraging barriers to movement to be strengthened. Similarly, a greater awareness of the linkages between trade and development problems might lead to trade liberalisation, but it could equally lead to the *regionalisation* of the world into tightly controlled trading blocs.

The HDI also serves to remind us that there is more to development than GNP. The differences in rankings on GNP compared with rankings on HDI for certain countries show the value of including as many indicators as possible. In Sri Lanka and Tanzania, for instance,

TABLE 2.1
The Human Development Index and Some Other Indicators, Selected Countries, 1992

Country	HDI	GNP pc (US $)	Rank on HDI	Rank on GNP pc	Rank out of 160 countries HDI	Rank out of 160 countries GNP pc	Adult literacy rate 1990 (%)	Average annual inflation rate 1980-90 (%)	Life expectancy at birth 1990 (years)
Japan	0.981	25 430	1	1	2	3	99.0	1.5	78.6
UK	0.962	16 100	2	3	10	21	99.0	5.8	75.7
Germany	0.955	22 320	3	2	12	10	99.0	2.7	75.2
Rep. of Korea	0.871	5 400	4	6	34	39	96.3	5.1	70.1
Singapore	0.848	11 160	5	4	40	25	88.0	1.7	74.0
Brazil	0.739	2 680	6	7	59	54	81.1	284.3	65.6
Saudi Arabia	0.687	7 050	7	5	67	33	62.4	-4.2	64.5
Thailand	0.685	1 420	8	8	69	79	93.0	3.4	66.1
Sri Lanka	0.651	470	9	10	76	120	88.4	11.1	70.9
China	0.612	370	10	11	79	130	73.3	5.8	70.1
Cameroon	0.313	960	11	9	118	88	54.1	5.6	53.7
Tanzania	0.268	110	12	14	126	158	65.0	25.8	54.0
Uganda	0.192	220	13	13	133	141	48.3	107.0	52.0
Sierra Leone	0.062	240	14	12	159	145	20.7	56.1	42.0

GNP lags behind HDI; whereas the reverse is true for Saudi Arabia and Cameroon. The Sri Lankans have an official GNP of $470 per head, but purchasing power of $2000 per head because goods are cheap; their life expectancy is 71 years, and 88 per cent of them are literate. That gives them an HDI rank of 76. Brazilians with GNP of $2680 per head have a purchasing power of $4300, can expect to live for 66 years, and 81 per cent of them are literate. They get an HDI rank of 59. This puts Sri Lanka significantly closer to Brazil on the HDI than on the basis of GNP per capita alone. Saudi Arabia with GNP of $7050 per head, purchasing power of $8300, life expectancy of 62 years and 62 per cent literacy plummets down the rankings from 33 to 67 when HDI is used instead of GNP per capita. Another useful potential aspect of the HDI is that it can be used to indicate the quality of life for different groups in society, such as ethnic minorities or for men as opposed to women.

Examining the 'promotions' and 'relegations' when the GNP per head of groups of nations are compared with their HDI can be quite revealing. Most Arab nations have high GNPs, but also high death rates and low literacy rates (especially among women) and so move rapidly down the HDI league table. Over-militarised countries tend to have a lower literacy rate: Pakistan with 154 soldiers per 100 teachers has a literacy rate of 30 per cent; India, with a ratio of 28 to 100 has literacy of 43 per cent (on the other hand Nicaragua with 326 soldiers per 100 teachers during the time that figures were collected had a 72 per cent literacy rate). One of the countries on which the HDI reflects extremely well is Costa Rica. Purchasing power there is not very high; but its life expectancy is one of the highest in the world. It has no army, so the soldier/teacher ratio is zero, and adult literacy is 93 per cent.

The main problem with the HDI is that it is subjective. The weighting of purchasing power, life expectancy and literacy within the index is arbitrary, and the index does come up with some anomalies. Many people would disagree, for instance, that Singapore should be ranked behind Argentina, or that the Chile is the 'best' latin American country in which to live.

It would be a mistake to think that 'development' is a process which is confined to the LDCs (although it is crucial to them, because in many of them people lack even the basic requirements for a life of any quality). Development in its broadest sense is a process which can be identified and studied in any country in which it takes place, whether that country is India, Taiwan, South Africa, Russia or the USA.

Table 2.2 shows the main rankings from the 1993 Human Development Report. This report controversially argued that it is possible to regard the United States as three countries instead of one. It said that the black population shares so little of the benefits of US society that it would rank 30 places behind the white population on the HDI. The US Hispanic population would be 35 places behind, and below some of the Latin American countries such as Uruguay and Chile. This is relevant to our discussion of 'relative poverty' in Chapter 4. According to the 1993 HDR, 'Many of today's struggles are for more than political power, they are for access to the ordinary opportunities of life – land, water, work, living space, and basic social services.'

TABLE 2.2
Main HDI Rankings, 1993

Overall top-ranked countries	Top developing nations
1. Japan	1. Barbados
2. Canada	2. Hong Kong
3. Norway	3. Cyprus
4. Switzerland	4. Uruguay
5. Sweden	5. Trinidad and Tobago
6. United States	6. Bahamas
7. Australia	7. S Korea
8. France	8. Chile
9. Netherlands	9. Costa Rica
10. Britain	10. Singapore
11. Iceland	11. Brunei
12. Germany	12. Argentina
13. Denmark	13. Venezuela
14. Finland	14. Dominica
15. Austria	15. Kuwait
16. Belgium	16. Mexico
17. New Zealand	17. Qatar
18. Luxembourg	18. Mauritius
19. Israel	19. Malaysia
	20. Bahrain
	21. Grenada
	22. Antigua and Barbuda

SOURCE UNDP, *Human Development Report.* 1993.

If development is a process which can be identified in any country, not just in LDCs, it follows that countries can experience *de-development* as well as *development*. The UNDP claims that despite the worldwide trend to more democracy, 90 per cent of the world's population have no control over institutions affecting their lives. Even in the richest areas of the world, a growing gap between rich people and poor people, or erosions of personal liberty, can be regarded as signs of de-development. Where economic policy appears to depend on the existence of an underclass of unemployed or lowly paid people, with little chance to participate in the decisions which affect their own lives, then many of the MDCs cannot be said to be properly developed. It is a sad comment on the decline of the UK as a manufacturing nation that the media have begun to comment on the existence of 'Third World' levels of poverty in some areas where unemployment is at significantly higher levels than the national average.

While the HDI is a fairly sophisticated average, it does omit some important components of the standard of living, in particular *environmental quality*. In *The Guardian's* 'Notes and Queries' column in March 1993 a reader asked whether it was true that Iceland had the highest standard of living in the world. Another reader supported this view, saying that Iceland has a classless society, where people build their own homes on their own land, and use central heating systems with water from natural hot springs. Electricity is generated by hydroelectric schemes, education is free, there is almost no unemployment, and Reykjavik has more bookshops per head of population than any other capital city. However, Professor David Pearce of University College London pointed out that although Iceland does do well in terms of the HDI, it is not at the top of the league table, and falls behind countries such as Japan and the USA. Professor Pearce leads a team of economists working on a measure of *sustainable development* – a green net national product (GNNP) – which gives more weight to environmental and conservation aspects of the quality of life.

Table 2.3 shows the occupants of the twenty 'top' and 'bottom' places in the 1997 HDI league table, together with twenty highest ranked 'medium' human development countries.

The 1997 report took *poverty* as its theme, and claimed that although progress in the twentieth century in reducing poverty has been 'remarkable and unprecedented', advances have been uneven and marred by setbacks, so that 'poverty remains pervasive'. It

TABLE 2.3
Human Development Index, Extracts, 1997

HDI rank	Life expectancy at birth (years) 1994	Adult literacy rate (%) 1994	Combined first-, second- and third-level gross enrolment ratio (%) 1994	Real GDP per capita (PPP$) 1994	Adjusted real GDP per capita (PPP$) 1994	Life expectancy index	Education index	GDP index	Human development index (HDI) value 1994	Real GDP per capita (PPP$) rank minus HDI rank
High human development	74.6	97.0	80	17,052	6,040	0.83	0.91	0.98	0.907	–
1 Canada	79.0	99.0	100	21,459	6,073	0.90	0.99	0.99	0.960	7
2 France	78.7	99.0	89	20,510	6,071	0.89	0.96	0.99	0.946	13
3 Norway	77.5	99.0	92	21,346	6,073	0.88	0.97	0.99	0.943	6
4 USA	76.2	99.0	96	26,397	6,101	0.85	0.98	0.99	0.942	–1
5 Iceland	79.1	99.0	83	20,566	6,071	0.90	0.94	0.99	0.942	9
6 Netherlands	77.3	99.0	91	19,238	6,067	0.87	0.96	0.99	0.940	13
7 Japan	79.8	99.0	78	21,581	6,074	0.91	0.92	0.99	0.940	0
8 Finland	76.3	99.0	97	17,417	6,041	0.85	0.98	0.98	0.940	15
9 New Zealand	76.4	99.0	94	16,851	6,039	0.86	0.97	0.98	0.937	15
10 Sweden	78.3	99.0	82	18,540	6,064	0.89	0.93	0.99	0.936	11
11 Spain	77.6	97.1	90	14,324	6,029	0.88	0.95	0.98	0.934	19
12 Austria	76.6	99.0	87	20,667	6,072	0.86	0.95	0.99	0.932	1
13 Belgium	76.8	99.0	86	20,985	6,072	0.86	0.95	0.99	0.932	–1
14 Australia	78.1	99.0	79	19,285	6,068	0.89	0.92	0.99	0.931	4
15 United Kingdom	76.7	99.0	86	18,620	6,065	0.86	0.95	0.99	0.931	5
16 Switzerland	78.1	99.0	76	24,967	6,098	0.88	0.91	0.99	0.930	–12
17 Ireland	76.3	99.0	88	16,061	6,037	0.85	0.95	0.98	0.929	8
18 Denmark	75.2	99.0	89	21,341	6,073	0.84	0.96	0.99	0.927	–8
19 Germany	76.3	99.0	81	19,675	6,069	0.86	0.93	0.99	0.924	–3
20 Greece	77.8	96.7	82	11,265	5,982	0.88	0.92	0.97	0.923	15

Medium human development	67.1	82.6	64	3.352	3.352	0.70	0.76	0.54	0.667	—
65 Lebanon	69.0	92.0	75	4,863	4,863	0.73	0.86	0.79	0.794	8
66 Suriname	70.7	92.7	71	4,711	4,711	0.76	0.85	0.76	0.792	10
67 Russian Federation	65.7	98.7	78	4,828	4,828	0.68	0.92	0.78	0.792	7
68 Brazil	66.4	82.7	72	5,362	5,362	0.69	0.79	0.87	0.783	0
69 Bulgaria	71.1	93.0	66	4,533	4,533	0.77	0.84	0.73	0.780	9
70 Iran, Islamic Rep. of	68.2	68.6	68	5,766	5,766	0.72	0.68	0.94	0.780	-9
71 Estonia	69.2	99.0	72	4,294	4,294	0.74	0.90	0.69	0.776	8
72 Ecuador	69.3	89.6	72	4,626	4,626	0.74	0.84	0.75	0.775	5
73 Saudi Arabia	70.3	61.8	56	9,338	5,953	0.76	0.60	0.97	0.774	-32
74 Turkey	68.2	81.6	63	5,193	5,193	0.72	0.75	0.84	0.772	-4
75 Korea, Dem. People's Rep. of	71.4	95.0	75	3,965	3,965	0.77	0.88	0.64	0.765	10
76 Lithuania	70.1	98.4	70	4,011	4,011	0.75	0.89	0.65	0.762	8
77 Croatia	71.3	97.0	67	3,960	3,960	0.77	0.87	0.64	0.760	10
78 Syrian Arab Rep.	67.8	69.8	64	5,397	5,397	0.71	0.68	0.87	0.755	-12
79 Romania	69.5	96.9	62	4,037	4,037	0.74	0.85	0.65	0.748	3
80 Macedonia, FYR	71.7	94.0	60	3,965	3,965	0.78	0.83	0.64	0.748	5
81 Tunisia	68.4	65.2	67	5,319	5,319	0.72	0.66	0.86	0.748	-12
82 Algeria	67.8	59.4	66	5,442	5,442	0.71	0.62	0.88	0.737	-17
83 Jamaica	73.9	84.4	65	3,816	3,816	0.82	0.78	0.61	0.736	7
84 Jordan	68.5	85.5	66	4,187	4,187	0.73	0.79	0.68	0.730	-3

TABLE 2.3 *(contd.)*

HDI rank	Life expectancy at birth (years) 1994	Adult literacy rate (%) 1994	Combined first-, second- and third-level gross enrolment ratio (%) 1994	Real GDP per capita (PPP$) 1994	Adjusted real GDP per capita (PPP$) 1994	Life expectancy index	Education index	GDP index	Human development index (HDI) value 1994	Real GDP per capita (PPP$) rank minus HDI rank
Low human development	56.1	49.9	47	1,308	1,308	0.52	0.49	0.20	0.403	–
156 Haiti	54.4	44.1	29	896	896	0.49	0.39	0.13	0.338	5
157 Angola	47.2	42.5	31	1,600	1,600	0.37	0.39	0.25	0.335	-24
158 Sudan	51.0	44.8	31	1,084	1,084	0.43	0.40	0.16	0.333	-4
159 Uganda	40.2	61.1	34	1,370	1,370	0.25	0.52	0.21	0.328	-19
160 Senegal	49.9	32.1	31	1,596	1,596	0.41	0.32	0.25	0.326	-26
161 Malawi	41.1	55.8	67	694	694	0.27	0.60	0.10	0.320	7
162 Djibouti	48.8	45.0	20	1,270	1,270	0.40	0.37	0.19	0.319	-16
163 Guinea-Bissau	43.2	53.9	29	793	793	0.30	0.46	0.11	0.291	1
164 Chad	47.0	47.0	25	700	700	0.37	0.40	0.10	0.288	2
165 Gambia	45.6	37.2	34	939	939	0.34	0.36	0.14	0.281	-5

166 Mozambique	46.0	39.5	25	986	986	0.35	0.35	0.15	0.281	-9
167 Guinea	45.1	34.8	24	1,103	1,103	0.34	0.31	0.17	0.271	-14
168 Eritrea	50.1	25.0	24	960	960	0.42	0.25	0.14	0.269	-9
169 Burundi	43.5	34.6	31	698	698	0.31	0.33	0.10	0.247	-2
170 Ethiopia	48.2	34.5	18	427	427	0.39	0.29	0.05	0.244	4
171 Mali	46.6	29.3	17	543	543	0.36	0.25	0.07	0.229	1
172 Burkina Faso	46.4	18.7	20	796	796	0.36	0.19	0.11	0.221	-9
173 Niger	47.1	13.1	15	787	787	0.37	0.14	0.11	0.206	-8
174 Rwanda	22.6	59.2	37	352	352	0.00	0.52	0.04	0.187	1
175 Sierra Leone	33.6	30.3	28	643	643	0.14	0.30	0.09	0.176	-4
All developing countries	61.8	69.7	56	2,904	2,904	0.61	0.65	0.46	0.576	–
Least developed countries	50.4	48.1	36	965	965	0.42	0.44	0.14	0.336	–
Sub-Saharan Africa	50.0	55.9	42	1,377	1,377	0.42	0.51	0.21	0.380	–
Industrial countries	74.1	98.5	83	15,986	6,037	0.82	0.93	0.98	0.911	–
World	63.2	77.1	60	5,798	5,798	0.64	0.71	0.94	0.764	–

SOURCE UNDP. *Human Development Report, 1997.*

argued that unfettered free-market economics generates inequality, and that positive government action is necessary to redress gender imbalances and to encourage 'pro-poor growth'. According to the UNDP *globalisation* offers great opportunities, but only if it is managed more carefully, and with a 'concern for global equity'; and special international action is required for special situations, to reduce the debts of the poorest countries, to increase their share of aid, and to open agricultural markets for their exports. The report also introduced a 'Human Poverty Index' which is further discussed in Chapter 3.

How and Why does Development Take Place?

By observing the experiences of today's MDCs in their earlier stages of development, and by following the progress of some of the more rapidly changing LDCs of today, we can attempt to analyse the main causes of and obstacles to development.

Accumulation of physical capital

Capital can be defined as 'wealth which can be used to produce further wealth'. It is a factor of production which is man made, and its essential purpose is to increase the productivity of the other factors of production, namely land, labour and enterprise. The process of purchasing and accumulating capital is known as *investment*. For investment to take place, a country's population must be prepared in the short run to reduce consumption and increase saving. Capital goods are not required as an end in themselves, but because they are used to produce consumer goods, which are the final products that people actually want.

In Chapter 1 we discussed the use of the production possibility curve which can be used to demonstrate the opportunity cost of investment in capital. Capital accumulation involves a short-term 'sacrifice', in that a population has to defer its consumption until a point in the future when its capital goods come 'on stream' and create consumer goods at a higher level than before. This promise of a long-term improvement in living standards is the 'reward' for this deferment.

There are two broad types of capital accumulation:

1. investment in physical capital
2. investment in human capital.

Physical capital includes factory buildings, machinery, shops, offices, vehicles; the aforementioned can be referred to as *business capital.* Items such as schools, roads, hospitals, and houses can be described as *social capital.*

FIGURE 2.1
Spending on Education

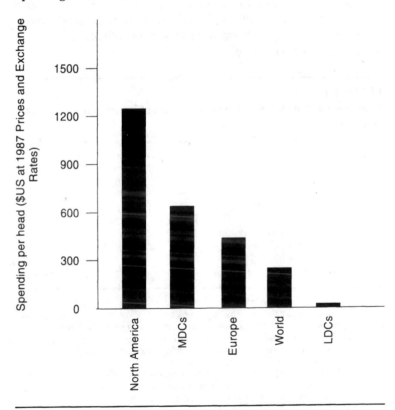

SOURCE UNICEF, *Children First,* Autumn 1992.

In the process of development, we can identify two broad patterns of capital accumulation. *Capital widening* occurs when extra capital is combined with an increased amount of labour, but the capital per worker does not change. Thus productivity (output per worker) is likely to remain static. *Capital deepening* involves an increase in the amount of capital per worker. This is often linked to innovation and technological change, including improved organisation and management techniques, improved communications, computerisation, mechanisation and so on. If successful, capital deepening will lead to increases in labour productivity.

Human capital is the accumulated knowledge, skills and attitudes of the working population. It also encompasses the physical, mental and social health of a nation. Education, health and training are often wrongly regarded as part of a country's *social welfare* system, rather than as *economic* issues with implications for growth and development. Countries which neglect human investment are unlikely to develop as rapidly as they otherwise could.

TABLE 2.4
Education as Investment: Economic Rates of Return on Education (per cent)

	Level of education		
Country group	*Primary*	*Secondary*	*Higher*
Industrial market economies (ten countries)	15[a]	11	11
Developing country exporters of manufactures [b]	15	13	9
Other developing countries (twenty-six countries)	28	17	14

NOTE   The economic rates of return (referred to as social rates of return in the literature on the economics of education) on which these averages are based are from studies which for the most part refer to the 1970s and early 1980s. For comparison, economic rates of return to investment in physical capital averaged 13 per cent for developing countries and 11 per cent for industrial market economies.
[a] The lack of a control group of illiterates in the industrial market economies prevents a direct computation; the estimate is based on the return for developing country exporters of manufactures.
[b] India, Israel, Singapore and Yugoslavia.
SOURCE   World Bank, *World Development Report* (1987).

Human resource development

A common error, in the MDCs as well as the LDCs, is to regard expenditure on such things as education, health and social facilities as acts of *consumption*, rather than properly viewing them as important components of *investment*.

Figure 2.1 and tables 2.4 and 2.5 refer to investment in what is sometimes called 'human capital'. Economists nowadays generally agree that investment of this sort is just as important, if not more important than investment in 'physical capital' (machinery, infrastructure, etc.)

The development of resources is an empty and valueless exercise without top priority being given to the development of human resources. What is development for, if it is not aimed at improving the human condition? Probably the greatest threat to human resource development at the present time is that of a too-rapid rise in population. This therefore constitutes a major obstacle to development, and is further discussed in Chapter 3. The related issues of poverty and the distribution of resources are discussed in Chapter 4.

Food production

In the poorest LDCs, the first priority is usually to increase food production, and so investment and technological change need to be geared first and foremost to agricultural techniques. Only when a population is adequately fed is it possible to diversify an economy into the secondary (industrial) and tertiary (service) sectors.

It should not be assumed that economic development automatically solves food-related problems simply by boosting production. Some countries, not all of which are generally described as LDCs have severe problems with food *distribution* as opposed to food production (witness the famous bread queues in Russia, for instance); while some of the systems in use in the richer MDCs (such as the Common Agricultural Policy of the European Union) create a tremendous wastage of food, and are thus economically inefficient because of the way in which they misallocate resources. Chapter 5 discusses some of the issues involved in food production in more detail.

TABLE 2.5
Spending on Social Capital

HDI rank	Social security benefits expenditure (as % of GDP) 1993	Percentage of central government expenditure on							
		Social security and welfare		Housing and community amenities		Health		Education	
		1980[a]	1992–95	1980[a]	1992–95	1980[a]	1992–95	1980[a]	1992–95
High human development	14.3	38.1	34.7	2.1	2.1	11.8	15.1	5.4	4.0
1 Canada	21.7	31.7	41.3	2.4	1.4	6.2	5.6	3.5	3.0
2 France	–	43.9	45.0	3.2	1.2	14.7	15.5	8.3	7.0
3 Norway	19.6	33.5	39.5	1.8	1.5	10.3	10.2	8.5	9.7
4 USA	10.5	34.2	29.6	2.6	2.7	10.7	18.3	2.5	1.6
5 Iceland	–	15.9	24.3	2.7	1.1	21.2	23.6	12.9	12.2
6 Netherlands	–	37.0	37.2	2.9	3.2	11.7	14.3	12.5	10.1
7 Japan	11.5	–	36.8	–	13.8	–	1.6	–	6.0
8 Finland	30.5	26.0	45.6	2.8	2.7	11.2	11.2	14.5	11.3
9 New Zealand	20.2	27.9	36.9	1.2	0.2	14.2	15.6	13.5	15.2
10 Sweden	38.3	46.4	48.2	3.1	5.4	2.0	0.2	10.5	5.0
11 Spain	–	59.0	39.0	1.5	0.5	0.6	6.2	7.7	4.4
12 Austria	24.5	45.1	45.8	3.3	2.7	13.2	13.2	9.6	9.5
13 Belgium	–	41.6	–	1.6	–	1.7	–	14.4	–
14 Australia	–	27.4	33.8	0.7	1.4	10.1	13.1	8.1	7.6
15 United Kingdom	–	28.3	29.6	2.5	2.9	13.2	14.0	2.2	3.3
16 Switzerland	14.0	48.3	–	0.8	–	12.7	–	3.3	–

17 Ireland	19.4	–	28.2	–	2.0	–	14.0	–	12.8
18 Denmark	29.5	41.2	39.9	2.1	1.8	1.4	1.1	10.0	10.6
19 Germany	24.7	49.5	–	0.4	0.6	19.2	16.8	0.8	0.8
20 Greece	–	30.6	13.4	2.5	1.3	10.5	7.4	9.6	8.5
21 Italy	–	31.4	24.5	1.0	–	10.8	–	9.1	–
23 Israel	11.8	13.7	50.8	0.2	5.8	3.5	5.7	8.5	13.6
27 Luxemburg	–	51.7	–	1.7	4.1	2.4	2.9	8.5	8.6
31 Portugal	9.0	24.6	–	0.7	–	10.4	–	10.3	–
34 Malta	–	35.6	34.0	1.2	7.4	9.7	12.1	8.0	12.4
35 Slovenia	11.1	–	–	–	–	–	–	–	–
39 Czech Rep.	13.3	–	28.1	–	1.2	–	16.7	–	11.2
42 Slovakia	17.3	–	–	–	–	–	–	–	–
48 Hungary	17.0	20.7	28.7	1.7	–	2.7	7.9	1.8	3.3
58 Poland	12.0	–	–	–	–	–	–	–	–
62 Belarus	–	–	36.5	–	1.2	–	2.5	–	17.6
Medium human development	–	–	–	–	–	–	–	–	–
67 Russian Federation	19.8	–	28.5	–	–	–	1.4	–	3.2
69 Bulgaria	–	–	28.0	–	1.9	–	2.8	–	3.3
71 Estonia	–	–	30.0	–	3.9	–	16.9	–	8.8
76 Lithuania	–	–	37.5	–	(.)	–	4.7	–	7.0
77 Croatia	–	32.4	–	3.2	–	–	13.9	–	6.7
79 Romania	16.9	16.2	28.8	1.3	0.9	0.7	8.1	3.0	9.7
80 Macedonia, FYR	–	–	–	–	–	–	–	–	–
85 Turkmenistan	–	–	–	–	–	–	–	–	–
92 Latvia	9.1	36.7	36.7	–	(.)	–	6.1	–	14.5
93 Kazakstan	–	–	–	–	–	–	–	–	–
95 Ukraine	–	–	–	–	–	–	–	–	–

TABLE 2.5 (*contd.*)

	Social security benefits expenditure (as % of GDP)	Percentage of central government expenditure on							
		Social security and welfare		Housing and community amenities		Health		Education	
HDI rank	1993	1980[a]	1992–95	1980[a]	1992–95	1980[a]	1992–95	1980[a]	1992–95
100 Uzbekistan	–	–	–	–	–	–	–	–	–
102 Albania	–	–	–	–	–	–	–	–	–
103 Armenia	–	–	–	–	–	–	–	–	–
105 Georgia	5.5	–	–	–	–	–	–	–	–
107 Kyrgyzstan	3.1	–	–	–	–	–	–	–	–
110 Moldova, Rep. of	–	–	–	–	–	–	–	–	–
115 Tajikistan	–	–	–	–	–	–	–	–	–
All developing countries	–	–	–	–	–	–	–	–	–
Industrial countries	–	–	–	–	–	–	–	–	–
World	–	–	–	–	–	–	–	–	–
North America	11.4	34.2	29.6	2.6	2.7	10.7	18.3	2.5	1.6
Eastern Europe and CIS	–	–	–	–	–	–	–	–	–
Western and Southern Europe	–	42.5	42.1	1.8	1.5	12.3	13.3	7.4	5.4
OECD	14.0	38.2	34.4	2.1	2.0	11.8	15.1	5.5	4.0
European Union	–	40.6	39.0	1.9	1.7	12.5	13.5	6.6	4.9
Nordic countries	30.8	39.1	43.9	2.5	3.3	5.1	4.3	10.6	8.4

NOTES: [a] Data refer to 1980 or a year around 1980.

Missing figures indicate that some countries supply incomplete information, or even no information at all when the UNDP first requests such data; hopefully figures will become available in the future.

SOURCE: *Column 1*: ILO 1995a; *columns 2–9*: IMF, *Government Finance Statistics Yearbook* various editions; UNDP, *Human Development Report*, 1997.

Industrial and technological change

Industrialisation in the longer established MDCs such as the UK was linked to the growth of particular groups of industries, such as textiles, coal, and steel. However, 'development', as opposed to 'growth' entails a spill-over into other sectors as well. Thus the so-called 'industrial revolution' in Britain was, in fact an agricultural, transport, and social revolution as well, involving massive increases in food production, the rapid building of railways and other forms of communication, and changes in political and social structures which were needed to house, feed and educate a rapidly expanding population, and to keep a more urbanised population healthy with an infrastructure that included hospitals, water supplies and sewers. In the 1970s, oil-exporting countries were able to grow due to 'windfall' earnings based on one economic sector; whether all of these countries have *developed* in the broadest sense of the word is a moot point.

Comparing MDCs with LDCs we find that MDCs often are capable of producing a higher output per worker, even if they have the same amount of capital stock per head. This is because the type of capital in use in MDCs is likely to be technologically more advanced. For example, a factory in an LDC might have 1 machine per 10 workers, the same ratio as a factory in an MDC. But the MDC's machines could well be capable of operating at much faster speeds than those in the LDC. This is not to say that investment in the 'latest' technology will always be an appropriate strategy for an LDC. Development specialists increasingly believe that what is essential is an investment in *appropriate* technology, and this concept is further examined in Chapter 6, which also examines industrialisation as a development issue.

International relationships

We are living in an increasingly *interdependent* world. The economies of the most successful MDCs are *open* economies, which depend on the life blood of international trade in exports and imports. In recent years there has been a growing realisation that economic opportunities and problems do not stop at national borders, and that international action is needed to deal with them. Countries with an *outward-looking* (export promoting) economic strategy, such as Singapore,

Hong Kong, South Korea and Taiwan have generally experienced more rapid development than those with an *inward-looking* (self-sufficient) strategy, such as the planned economies of Russia and Eastern Europe. Outward-looking countries have been better placed to benefit from *comparative advantage* (See Chapter 7) and have not only created *more* income, but have also *diversified* – that is, created income in a wider variety of economic activities, rather than depending on a narrow range of goods and services.

Breakdowns in international relationships – a war being the most drastic example – are obvious barriers to development. Multinational enterprises are increasingly dominating the global economy, and the free movement of capital between the financial centres of the world has accelerated in the last decade, assisted by tremendous increases in the speed of telecommunication. The international organisation of labour has a long way to go to match the way in which capital and enterprise have organised themselves on a global scale. Trade unions organised on national lines are in a weak position when negotiating with companies which can make decisions affecting living standards in countries thousands of miles from their headquarters. The international activities of banks have had particularly profound effects on the well-being of people living in LDCs.

International trading relationships are increasingly being negotiated through international institutions, and organisations such as WTO can have an important influence on development. We take up some of these issues in Chapters 7 and 8.

Government and markets

Economics is fundamentally about the 'efficient' allocation of resources; one of the crucial issues facing the world today and being debated in MDCs and LDCs alike is the role of governments and markets in the allocation of resources. Some people, including very eminent economists, have a touching (almost religious) faith in the ability of either markets or governments to work their 'magic'; but out of the world of the ivory tower economics is not merely a set of mathematical relationships. Economic questions cannot be separated from questions about the type of society in which we wish to live. Thus the issue of governments versus markets can be seen as a question of balance, rather than a question of 'either/or'; as Jenny Wales has stated in a companion volume in this series (*Investigating Social Issues*), the comparison should be between an imperfect market and an imperfect government, not some ideal abstraction. Among the LDCs which have developed most rapidly in recent years we can detect at least some idea of 'partnership' between the enterprise economy and the state. It could further be argued that among the MDCs showing stagnation or decline over the last decade there has been too much reliance either on markets or on the state, and too little attention paid to the idea of a mixed economy. In Chapter 9 we examine some of the aspects of development which are best tackled by markets, and some which require government intervention for maximum economic efficiency.

Among the latter are some of the influences which affect the issue of whether development is *sustainable*; that is, whether it can continue in the long run without excessive external costs such as the loss of vital resources. Land degradation, deforestation, environmental pollution, global warming, and depletion of the ozone layer are all barriers to development which cannot be overcome by markets alone; they require government action, and international action at that.

Development Policy

In the preceding paragraphs we have raised a number of issues, some of which have been selected for further examination elsewhere in this book. It should be emphasised that there is no single key to development, no special mix of ingredients which will guarantee that an LDC can become an MDC, or prevent an MDC moving in the opposite direction. It follows that a country following a particular growth strategy cannot be guaranteed success; however, certain policy combinations do appear to have a greater chance of long-term sustained success than others.

Population Growth: Threat or Opportunity?

3

Does the growth of world population represent a threat or an opportunity? Is the development of a country helped or hindered by rapid population growth?

Supply and Demand

Population can be regarded in basic economic theory as one of the 'underlying conditions' of demand. Changes in the overall size of a country's population can be expected to increase the overall level of demand or, in the terminology of the economist, 'shift' demand to the right. Changes in the composition of the population (such as the ratio of older people to younger people) can affect the pattern of demand, and so shift the demand curves for particular products. In the case of the LDCs, the most obvious effects of population changes are on the demand for the basics of life, such as food, water, clothing and shelter. On the other hand, population can be seen as an underlying condition of supply. People are a 'natural resource', and economic theory tells us that an increase in a factor resource can result in an increase in the supply of goods and services. It is sometimes said that 'with every mouth God sends a pair of hands'. Is this a realistic proposition in the context of the food production of LDCs? Can an increase in population be used to increase output, and so shift to the right the supply curves for food, houses, and other necessities?

Population Pressures

Let us consider some facts and figures from UN sources. In 1972 there were less than 4 billion people living on this planet, of whom just over 70 per cent lived in LDCs. In 1990, the earth's population was over 5 billion, with nearly 80 per cent living in LDCs. And the number was growing faster than ever before. In the year 1000 BC the earth's population was about 100 million: this is the amount now being added to the population every year. Every single day, we share the resources of this planet with 250,000 people more than the day before.

FIGURE 3.1
World Population Projections

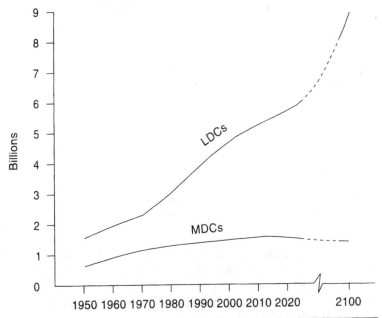

SOURCE   United Nations Development Programme, *Human Development Report,* 1991.

It took all the centuries from the dawn of civilisation for world population to reach 4 billion (in 1975); but UN estimates claim it will take only until 2020 for it to double to 8 billion, with nearly 90 per cent living in LDCs, the areas least able to cope with the resource consequences of increased numbers. Table 3.1 lists figures for what are expected to be the world's largest cities in the year 2000, and as they were in 1985.

In 1972 there were just three cities in the world with over 10 million inhabitants, only one of them in an LDC. Under 40 per cent of the world's population lived in cities. By 1992, there were 13 cities with over 10 million inhabitants, nine of them in LDCs. Over 45 per cent of the world population is urban: by 2000 this will rise to 50 per cent.

TABLE 3.1
The World's Largest Cities, 1985 and 2000

City	Millions (2000)	Millions (1985)	Ranking (2000)	Ranking (1985)
Mexico City	25.8	17.3	1	2
São Paulo	24.0	15.9	2	3
Tokyo	20.2	18.8	3	1
Calcutta	16.5	11.0	4	6
Bombay	16.0	10.1	5	11
New York	15.8	15.6	6	4
Shanghai	14.3	12.0	7	5
Seoul	13.8	10.3	8	10
Tehran	13.6	7.5	9	20
Rio de Janeiro	13.3	10.4	10	8
Jakarta	13.3	7.9	11	17
Delhi	13.2	7.4	12	21

SOURCE *United Nations Development Programme, Human Development Report,* 1991.

Urbanisation leads to local problems, one of which is homelessness. Shanty towns of cardboard boxes, wood and corrugated iron are a feature of most cities in the LDCs. Where the climate permits, people live on the streets where they are prey to crime and violence. In 1980 it was estimated that in Mexico City, 40 per cent of the population lived in squatter settlements, in Delhi it was 56 per cent.

In Addis Ababa the shanty population was $1\frac{1}{2}$ million, a staggering 85 per cent of the population.

Urbanisation also leads to new problems on an international level. The fact that Mexico City is choked with cars is not of purely local interest, if it contributes to global warming through depleting the ozone layer. In 1972 there were 250 million motor vehicles in the world, including 200 million cars. Their pollution was confined almost entirely to the MDCs. By 1992 there were just over 600 million motor vehicles, including 480 million cars. MDCs still had the great majority, but traffic-related air pollution was becoming a major problem in LDCs also. The former planned economies, moving towards the use of markets represent a huge pool of potential car consumers in the near future.

During 1972, 16 billion tonnes of carbon dioxide were released into the atmosphere from burning fossil fuels. During 1992, 23 billion tonnes were released.

All these problems are linked through the 'demand' side of the economy to the issue of *population growth*. The governments of LDCs are constantly seeking new ways of trying to reduce their population growth rates, but they are generally unsuccessful. Why is the population growth rate so high in poorer countries? What are the economic effects of rapid population growth? Are LDCs poor because they are overpopulated, or are they overpopulated because they are poor?

The Prophet of Doom

The Rev. Thomas Robert Malthus (1766–1834) was a contemporary of Adam Smith, and a close friend of David Ricardo. He is best remembered for his essays on population. Malthus suggested that (due to the fact that it takes two people to make a baby) population had a tendency to increase in a geometric progression:

2, 4, 8, 16, 32, 64, etc.

While population 'multiplied', food could only be 'added' to by cultivating extra land, and so food production could only be increased in arithmetic progression:

2, 4, 6, 8, 10, 12, etc.

It can be seen that within three 'generations' population out-strips food production. Is this inevitable, and if so, why?

Food production is subject to the *law of diminishing returns*, which states that if variable factors (such as labour) are combined with a fixed factor (such as a given amount of land), eventually the resulting increases in output (of food, for instance) will get progressively smaller. This law is one of the few economic laws which appears to hold true without exception. It is, however, a short-run law, which assumes that at least one of the factors of production is fixed. In the long run, when all factors are variable, *economies of scale* are possible, and this possibility was overlooked by Malthus.

Why does the law of diminishing returns operate? One way of looking at it is to say that factors of production are not perfect substitutes. When we apply variable factors such as seeds, water, fertiliser, and human labour to a fixed factor (land), we are doing so because we are short of land and are, in a sense, using the other factors as 'substitutes' for more land. After a certain point, it becomes physically and technologically impossible to obtain further output using the variable factors, and land is used beyond its capacity (the phrase 'blood from a stone' springs to mind). Consider what would happen if factors of production *were* perfect substitutes. Then it would be possible to apply wonder-fertilisers, amazing technology, and human ingenuity and effort to a small allotment, and feed the world with the resulting output!

The law of diminishing returns applies to all factors, not just land and labour. Each kilogram of fertiliser applied to the US corn belt or to an Asian rice paddy field boosts yields by only half as much as 20 years ago. MDCs use more pesticides than the LDCs, but the most rapid growth rate is in the LDCs. In 1980 the LDCs accounted for only 8 per cent of their use; by 1986 this had risen to 15 per cent. In the light of new scientific evidence, and under the spotlight of shifting public opinion, MDCs often ban certain pesticides at home, but continue to export them to the LDCs.

In order to feed a rapidly expanding population new land has to be cultivated for 'cash crops'. By 1972 up to a third of the earth's tropical rainforests had been destroyed, with a further 100 000 acres disappearing every year. By 1992 deforestation rates had risen to 170 000 acres per year. Seeking protein from the sea, 56 million tonnes of fish were taken from the oceans in 1972; by 1992 this had risen to 90 million tonnes, with many fish stocks at risk of total collapse.

Malthus argued that without restraints the higher output and living standards predicted by Adam Smith and other economists would not be sustained. Unless there was moral restraint on the size of families the outlook was gloomy: there would be famine, war and pestilence until the situation righted itself.

During the nineteenth century, however, Malthus's ideas were effectively sidelined by the industrial revolution in which Britain was a leading player. The huge investment in capital during Victorian times enabled this tiny island to support a vastly increased population without any obvious signs of diminishing returns setting in. There was investment in social capital (towns, cities, roads, houses) and in industrial capital (factories, machinery). Agriculture was as revolutionised as any other industrial sector, and huge gains in productivity resulted from new technology and improved techniques. Neither could Malthus have forseen that the vast crop fields of the American Midwest would make food exports available to the industrialising world on such a large scale.

The Case for Population Growth

The fact that an unprecedented explosion in population can be accompanied by a general rise in living standards has led some economists (sometimes described as 'pro-natalists') to argue that there is no population problem at all. People are as much a 'natural resource' as any other factor of production, and so why should a country fear an increase in this resource any more than it would fear the discovery of new oil reserves?

In the nineteenth century the USA encouraged the 'huddled masses' of Europe to settle in the New World; and in the recent past Australia very heavily subsidised immigrants: in the 1950s it was possible for a British family to travel to settle in Australia for a boat fare of £10.

If population size is too small in terms of land area, then a country's development can be retarded: Adam Smith himself argued that the benefits of specialisation are limited by the 'extent of the market', and not only factories but also roads, hospitals, schools and other items of social infrastructure can improve with increased population size and density. The idea of *optimum population* is a useful one: it is the level of population which enables a country to combine its labour force with other resources so as to maximise its output per person. It would be difficult to argue that most of today's LDCs are underpopulated, given their low levels of capital, and the fact that many of their population are lacking in the basics of nutrition, clothing and shelter, let alone the education and training that is needed to maximise output from a given set of resources.

The Case Against

An interesting piece of mathematics which is an approximation, but often comes in useful to economists is the 'Rule of 72'. If something is growing at x per cent per year, then to find how many years it will take for that something to double in size, divide x into 72. Let us say that at the moment the rate of growth of world population is 1.5 per cent. This means that world population will double in 48 years. This is a very short time in terms of human history; but remember that in LDCs the growth rate is twice as high. Unless something astonishing happens which even Malthus could never have predicted – as astonishing as, for instance, the creation of human settlements on Mars! – it is physically, economically and logically impossible for current population growth rates to continue. Predictions concerning the year 2000 are startling enough, but if we were to project current growth rates to the year 3000 we could envisage a world where every inhabitant has a square metre of land to stand on, or where the weight of people and the buildings they live in exceed the weight of the earth itself. Faced with such a nightmare it is clear that the arguments of the pro-natalists, while they might suit certain countries at certain times in their history, certainly cannot be applied to the world as a whole; neither do they apply to most of the LDCs, where 19 out of 20 births will occur over the next 40 years. Anyone who doubts this, or thinks that population is a distant problem only concerning people in far away countries, need only consider the social and political stresses and strains already being caused in some of the richest countries of the world by so called 'economic refugees' seeking a better life by migration, usually illegally, over national borders.

The Dependency Ratio

The size of a country's population depends on three variables: the birth rate, the death rate, and migration. As countries develop, the death rate can be expected to fall, due to medical and dietary improvements, and better living conditions. Education and the availability of contraceptives can also affect the average size of families, as can new opportunities for women, whose period of fertility can be reduced in effect by their engaging in employment. LDCs also dramatically reduce infant mortality as their living standards increase. These changes affect a country's dependency ratio.

Population growth results in an increase in the dependency ratio, i.e. the ratio of dependent to working people, mainly through an increase in the number of children. In MDCs, the tendency for the dependency ratio to increase due to an ageing population is largely cancelled by a static or falling birth rate. In LDCs the dependency ratio is over 40 per cent, and in many cases is higher than 50 per cent compared to 30 per cent in MDCs. In effect, this means that any addition to national income produced by a worker in an LDC has to support two persons, whereas in an MDC it supports $1\frac{1}{2}$ persons. It also means that a large amount of national resources has to be diverted towards basic consumption needs such as food and clothing rather than being invested. When investment takes place it has to be geared towards the needs of young persons, in the form of education and medical services. While such services are important, they might not contribute directly to productivity in the same way as industrial investment.

When children grow to reach working age, a country's capital stock has to serve a larger workforce; this is known as *capital shallowing*, and it results in a fall in productivity. Making just enough investment to keep pace is known as *capital widening*; a country achieving this will find itself spending more and more money just to stand still, and maintain its social and economic infrastructure. A country will only make further development if *capital deepening* is possible. If investment funds are difficult to come by, then factories, schools, roads, telecommunications, and so on, will stagnate, unless population growth is limited. A reduction in population growth can enable capital deepening to take place without significantly increasing the total amount of investment, borrowing and indebtedness.

Social Attitudes

Enough has already been said in this chapter to indicate that population growth is an important economic problem. But it is more than that: it is a social and political problem also. Why do poor people in poor countries have large families? One possibility is that they see children as a form of security for old age. If they know that infant mortality is high, then they will calculate that having a large family will ensure that at least some will survive into adulthood. It follows that population should not be tackled in isolation. Dumping lorry-loads of contraceptives in Latin American peasant villages is not the answer. There must be an improvement in social and economic conditions, together with welfare provisions which reduce people's need for children as potential breadwinners so that people can trust in reduced levels of infant mortality and begin to plan family sizes properly.

Population Control

Almost all LDCs use population control methods as part of their attempts to break out of the underdevelopment trap. These methods have two parts: the provision of cheap contraception facilities, and incentives to limit family size. In India, public opinion was turned against family planning when in the mid-1970s the Prime Minister Indhira Gandhi's son Sanjay headed a brutal project of enforced sterilisation. Now the emphasis in India is on voluntary family planning, and a wide range of methods. While there are stories of government officials offering transistor radios to men who agreed to have a vasectomy, the greatest successes occur, as in so many other spheres of development economics, where the emphasis is on education. In many sections of society men are under the impression that condoms are only appropriate for use with prostitutes. Despite such taboos, the Indian government has estimated that between 1951 and 1991 its national family programme has averted some 130 million births. Nevertheless, 49 babies were still being born in India every minute; 17 million being added every year.

Where population programmes pay insufficient regard to deep-seated prejudices and cultures, there can be quite horrific side-effects. In China, where families are discouraged from having more than one child, it is said that there is a high incidence of infanticide, because social pressures to have a son causes fathers to murder their baby daughters.

The influence of the Roman Catholic church over many of the LDCs, particularly those in Latin America, is also an issue which needs to be addressed by the promoters of population programmes. What needs to be borne in mind is the urgency of the problems ahead. After the year 2000, the lower and higher projections of population diverge more and more rapidly. That means that governments and international organisations must act immediately. Fertility must fall during the 1990s if growth rates are to fall in the 21st century. According to the International Planned Parenthood Federation (IPPF) which met in October 1992 in New Delhi, for lower population projections to come to pass, contraceptive use would have to rise this decade by 50 per cent, from 387 million to 567 million couples. According to one delegate, the cost of the contraceptives would be $5 billion, and the total cost of family planning services would be $9 billion a year, which he compared with global military spending which he put at $2 billion a day, or $730 billion a year.

Children in the Population

In 1989 the United Nations General Assembly approved a Convention on the Rights of the Child. The 54 articles of the convention outline three types of rights:

1. *Provision* means that children have rights to be provided with such things as a name, a nationality, education, play, culture and religion.
2. *Protection* means that children should be protected from things which are harmful such as abuse, separation from parents, or commercial exploitation.
3. *Participation* means that a child should take part in making decisions which will affect his or her life.

The overall objective is to give children their own version of the 'freedoms' embodied in the 1948 UN Declaration of Human Rights, with the aim of ensuring that children can prepare for adulthood with the right to 'survive and develop'.

The UN Convention on the Rights of the Child has now been rati-
fied by 126 countries with very different cultures and economies.
These countries are now obliged to work towards standards of services
recommended by the convention, such as in education and in health,
and have to produce reports on the progress being made (the UK's
first report was published during 1994).

FIGURE 3.2
Infant Mortality Rate (Children under 5)

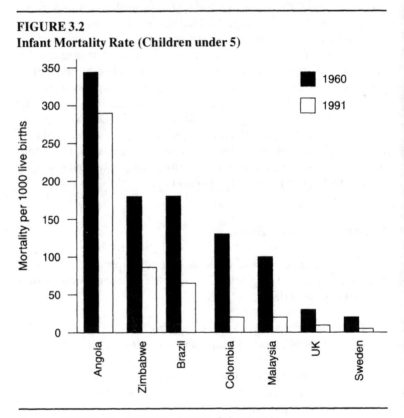

SOURCE UNICEF, *The State of the World's Children*, 1993.

It is estimated that over the world 155 million children live in poverty, and over 14 million die each year from illnesses. Only 50 per
cent of the world's children are immunised against major childhood
diseases, and 4 million children die each year from diarrhoea linked
to malnutrition and poor quality drinking water. 100 million children

live on city streets, and 50 million children under the age of 15 work full time, in some countries as coal miners and even as soldiers.

FIGURE 3.3
Main Causes of Death of Children under 5, in Developing Countries 1990

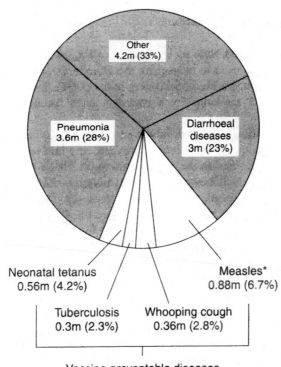

Vaccine-preventable diseases

*Including measles with diarrhoeal disease and measles with pneumoria

---

Source   UNICEF, *The State of the World's Children*, 1993.

According to the United Nations Children's Fund (UNICEF), meeting the needs of all the world's children for adequate nutrition, clean water, basic health care and primary education would cost about £16 billion a year. This is a little more than twice the amount borrowed by the UK government in September 1992 in its abortive attempt to support the pound in the European Exchange Rate Mechanism, and nearly fifty times smaller than global military spending. That such sums are so relatively small, in global terms, leads to the conclusion that any shortfall in food and other basic provision, for children at least, is due more to the lack of political will rather than a lack of money.

The Human Poverty Index

In 1997 the United Nations Development Programme adapted the three indicators used in measuring the Human Development Index (HDI) to produce a Human Poverty Index (HPI). These indicators (see Chapter 2) are longevity, knowledge, and a decent living standard.

Table 3.2 shows the HPI ranking for developing countries, and compares this 'qualitative' index of poverty (the HPI) with a 'quantitative' index (known as the $-a-day measure). That is to say, it compares an index which looks at more than monetary measures with one which concentrates solely on monetary measures. The $-a-day index, as its name suggests, measures the average number of dollars at the disposal of a member of the population for subsistence purposes each day, whereas the HPI measures the access – or more accurately the lack of access – that the poor have to the basic essentials to the quality of life. A higher HPI index indicates greater poverty.

The HPI serves as a useful complement to income measures of poverty, and reminds us that eradicating poverty involves not only increasing the incomes of the poor, but also increasing their access to basic services such as education, housing and health care. The HDI and HPI are complementary, and should be studied in conjunction with each other, the former showing how not only income but also other measures when conglomerated add to human welfare; the latter showing how being deprived of these factors creates poverty among a proportion of the population.

The Development Trap

In domestic economics, the 'poverty trap' is a situation in which some families are kept in poverty by a kind of vicious circle. If they try to find employment, or they seek a higher-paid job, then they move into a higher tax band which together with the loss of welfare benefits, can leave them worse off than before. Some economists have suggested that in international terms, there is such a thing as an *underdevelopment trap*. This is where a low level of capital per worker results in low productivity. This low productivity results in low output per worker. Low output per worker results in low income per head, low levels of saving, low levels of investment, and low levels of productivity. Thus the cycle of low income and low productivity reinforces itself.

TABLE 3.2
HPI Ranking for Developing Countries, 1997

Country	Human poverty Index (HPI) value (%)	HPI rank	HPI rank minus HDI rank	HPI rank minus $1-a-day poverty rank
Trinidad and Tobago	4.1	1	−4	−
Cuba	5.1	2	−18	−
Chile	5.4	3	1	−13
Singapore	6.6	4	3	−
Costa Rica	6.6	5	2	−15
Colombia	10.7	6	−3	−6
Mexico	10.9	7	−1	−9
Jordan	10.9	8	−11	1
Panama	11.2	9	2	−13
Uruguay	11.7	10	6	−
Thailand	11.7	11	1	6
Jamaica	12.1	12	−6	1
Mauritius	12.5	13	2	−
United Arab Emirates	14.9	14	8	−
Ecuador	15.2	15	1	−15
Mongolia	15.7	16	−12	−
Zimbabwe	17.3	17	−24	−18
China	17.5	18	−11	−12
Philippines	17.7	19	−7	−9
Dominican Rep.	18.3	20	−1	−5
Libyan Arab Jamahiriya	18.8	21	9	−
Sri Lanka	20.7	22	−1	8
Indonesia	20.8	23	−4	3
Syrian Arab Rep.	21.7	24	9	−
Honduras	22.0	25	−8	−15

TABLE 3.2 *(contd.)*

Country	Human poverty Index (HPI) value (%)	HPI rank	HPI rank minus HDI rank	HPI rank minus $1-a-day poverty rank
Bolivia	22.5	26	−6	9
Iran, Islamic Rep. of	22.6	27	14	–
Peru	22.8	28	6	−14
Botswana	22.9	29	4	−8
Paraguay	23.2	30	6	–
Tunisia	24.4	31	15	15
Kenya	26.1	32	−14	−13
Viet Nam	26.2	33	−4	–
Nicaragua	27.2	34	−5	−7
Lesotho	27.5	35	−13	−12
El Salvador	28.0	36	5	–
Algeria	28.6	37	20	21
Congo	29.1	38	−4	–
Iraq	30.7	39	1	–
Myanmar	31.2	40	−3	–
Cameroon	31.4	41	−4	–
Papua New Guinea	32.0	42	2	–
Ghana	32.6	43	−1	–
Egypt	34.8	44	14	15
Zambia	35.1	45	−8	−14
Guatemala	35.5	46	12	−9
India	36.7	47	−2	–
Rwanda	37.9	48	−29	−2
Togo	39.3	49	−7	–
Tanzania, U. Rep. of	39.7	50	−8	14
Lao People's Dem. Rep.	40.1	51	4	–
Zaire	41.2	52	0	–
Uganda	41.3	53	−13	−3
Nigeria	41.6	54	3	9
Morocco	41.7	55	19	30
Central African Rep.	41.7	56	−4	–
Sudan	42.2	57	−8	–
Guinea–Bissau	43.6	58	−11	−8
Namibia	45.1	59	24	–
Malawi	45.8	60	−8	–
Haiti	46.2	61	−3	–
Bhutan	46.3	62	−1	–
Côte d'Ivoire	46.3	63	8	18
Pakistan	46.8	64	14	24

Mauritania	47.1	65	6	11
Yemen	47.6	66	9	–
Bangladesh	48.3	67	13	–
Senegal	48.7	68	1	0
Burundi	49.0	69	–3	–
Madagascar	49.5	70	9	–1
Guinea	50.0	71	0	19
Mozambique	50.1	72	2	–
Cambodia	52.5	73	11	–
Mali	54.7	74	0	–
Ethiopia	56.2	75	2	14
Burkina Faso	58.3	76	1	–
Sierra Leone	59.2	77	–1	–
Niger	66.0	78	2	3

NOTE   HDI and $1-a-day poverty ranks have been recalculated for the universe of 78 countries. A negative number indicates that the country performs better on the HPI than on the other measure, a positive the opposite.

SOURCE   Human Development Report Office and World Bank 1996; UNDP, 1997.

The Malthusian Trap

The Malthusian trap is a variant of the development trap idea. Here, low productivity results from the capital shallowing process described earlier. Because a country is poor, its population growth is large; because its population growth is large, its productivity is low; because its productivity is low, its income is low; because its income is low its population is large, and so on.

We began the chapter with the question of whether large populations cause poverty or poverty causes large populations. The answer is that they both feed off each other. The experience of MDCs is that economic development is the best form of contraception. While it cannot be argued that higher income standards automatically reduce birth rates, and while it might not be that overpopulation is the only cause of poverty, it is undeniable that better living standards can have a beneficial effect on population growth. A way has to be found out of the development trap of rapid population growth, capital shallowing, low productivity, and rapid population growth. Unless the vicious circle can be broken, the name of Malthus is destined to become even more well known than it was during his lifetime.

Cities such as São Paulo, Mexico City and Nairobi provide stark evidence to anyone who doubts the seriousness of the effects of rapid population growth and growing divisions between rich and poor. Where markets fail to house, feed and educate the population – so that while the 'have-nots' live in the streets the 'haves' imprison themselves behind grids and electric fences – it is clear that if development is to be sustainable, then international action by governments acting together is urgently needed to tackle what is arguably the single most urgent problem facing mankind. Exponential population growth is literally a matter of life and death.

Can We Cure Poverty?

What do we mean by 'poverty'? Can poverty be cured? In 1990 the World Bank published a report on global poverty in which it said that for the poor the 1980s could be described as a 'lost decade'.

Who Are the Poor?

Relative poverty is defined as a living standard which falls well below the average of the country in question. International organisations such as the European Union (EU) and the Organisation for Economic Cooperation and Development (OECD) regularly publish statistics showing the numbers of people who have incomes which are less than half of the average for their nation.

An alternative approach, as used by the World Bank, is to measure *absolute poverty*, defined as a level of income required to purchase some of the minimum requirements of life, such as a given number of calories. The World Bank places its 'poverty line' at $370 (approximately £200) per year. Most citizens of MDCs would find it difficult to even begin to imagine what life would be like on an income of $370 per year, but even with the poverty line set at this very low level, we find that in 1985 there were 1125 million people living in poverty, an increase of 355 million over 1975. The

World Development Report (WDR) of 1990 admitted that past policies had failed to reduce poverty, and that even if all the most ambitious targets set out in the WDR were achieved, there would still be 700 million people living in poverty in the year 2000. More realistically, the WDR hoped that the number of poor could fall to 825 million, depending on how committed the governments of both the developing and developed world were to policies aimed at reducing poverty.

TABLE 4.1
Poverty in LDCs

Region	Percentage of world's population	Percentage of world's poor	Millions of poor 1985	Millions of poor 2000
East Asia	40.2	25.0	525	365
South Asia	29.7	46.4	180	265
Latin America and Caribbean	11.2	6.6	280	70
Sub-Saharan Africa	11.1	16.1	65	65
Europe, Middle East and North Africa	7.7	5.9	75	60

NOTE   Forecast for year 2000 dependent on implementation of World Bank Recommendations.
SOURCE   World Bank, *World Development Report*, 1990.

According to the WDR, nearly half the world's poor people live in South Asia, while roughly half the people of sub-Saharan Africa and South Asia are poor. One third of the population of the LDCs are living on less than $370 per year. Life expectancy in sub-Saharan Africa is 50 years, while in Japan it is 80. Mortality among children under 5 in South Asia exceeds 170 deaths per 1000 people, while in Sweden it is fewer than 10. More than 110 million people in LDCs have no access to primary education. Women are a deprived and powerless underclass in many countries. Poverty is severest in rural areas, and agriculture is the main source of income for most of the world's poor, although urban poverty is a worsening problem. In Venezuela, for instance, 85 per cent of the poor live in urban areas; in Brazil 75 per cent of the urban poor have jobs in the 'unofficial' economy, and these are jobs where wage rates are likely to be very low.

Too Poor to Live?

Keynesian economics suggests that the average propensity to consume (the fraction of income spent on consumption of goods and services) increases as income decreases, and the findings of the WDR are consistent with this idea. Poor households tend to be large, and spend most of their income on consumption.

How to Cure Poverty?

In the 1950s and 1960s the MDCs saw the main way of reducing world poverty as being through economic growth. In the 1970s, the provision of health, nutritional services and education were seen as more important. In its 1980 survey of poverty the World Bank argued that improvements in social services would direct income growth towards the poor. During the 1960s and 1970s there was some progress in reducing world poverty, but in the 1980s there was less success. Many LDCs suffered directly from world recession, while aid recipients were hit by constraints on public spending in the donor countries which affected aid programmes. Meanwhile, debt crises caused macroeconomic shocks as poorer countries found that they could not pay their debts through current output, but had to borrow in order to repay previous debts. The WDR suggests that poverty has been reduced most successfully where countries have followed a two-part strategy.

The first part involves poor countries achieving economic growth through the use of *appropriate technology*. Generally, such technology is labour-intensive rather than capital intensive and thus makes use of the abundant resource of a poor country, its labour. Countries such as Indonesia and Sri Lanka give incentives towards agricultural techniques and manufacturing employing large numbers, together with basic infrastructure such as road-building.

The second part consists of providing poor countries with a range of social services, including basic health care and elementary education. Family planning is a vital area, and in countries where family planning programmes have been successfully implemented poverty has declined sharply.

Aid and Absolute Poverty

International aid is not always effective in reducing poverty. Indeed, donor countries rarely consider the reduction of poverty to be an important reason for supplying aid, and so the aid funds tend to be channelled into sectors within the poor countries where power and influence is already concentrated: in other words, aid fails to reach the people in greatest need. The World Bank, on the other hand, considers that aid should be channelled to those countries whose governments have a clear commitment to reducing poverty, and that at least some of the aid should be specifically targeted towards the least advantaged people within those countries.

The World Bank estimates that poverty (on its absolute measure) could be virtually eliminated in East Asia by the end of the century, but that it could increase in sub-Saharan Africa. While it expects the overall figure in Europe, the Middle East and North Africa to remain the same, its composition will change, with Eastern Europe causing particular problems as the role of the state changes, and as some states disintegrate. In 1990 the World Bank was reasonably optimistic that Eastern Europe would be able to eliminate absolute poverty through a rapid transition to a market system, together with social security safety nets providing for workforces losing their jobs. The subsequent descent of certain states into civil war makes the prospects much more gloomy.

Poverty and the Environment

Environmental degradation is both a cause of poverty, and is caused by poverty. For many of the world's poorest people the 'environment' is their very means of survival: forests, rivers, land, are what they rely upon for their basic needs. When countries become involved with international institutions, multinational companies, or international bankers, they often find their economy becoming skewed towards cash crops and export-orientated agriculture. Results include the loss of rainforests and desertification to produce an environment unable to support its population.

International action is needed to encourage a fairer world trading system centred on basic needs, responsible interaction with the environment, employment for the poor, fair and stable prices, sounder investment patterns with training, appropriate technology and aid which empowers the poor rather than entrenching domination by the rich: in short, there needs to be some sort of justice for the world's poor. A great problem is that economists are not very good at discussing concepts such as 'justice' or 'fairness'; however, even the most positive of positive economists can arrive at policy recommendations likely to have the effects described above. 'Enlightened self-interest' suggests that developed trading nations, short of markets for their exports, can benefit from sustainable growth among the impoverished nations; and the serious environmental implications of world poverty should help ensure that the developed world will wake up to the fact that we are all involved: poverty is not always someone else's problem.

Relative Poverty

In our definition of development we have drawn attention to the importance of attaining a more equal distribution of income and wealth. Relative poverty is a much more difficult concept to pin down and measure than absolute poverty, as it involves making comparisons of people's living standards both within and between countries; and as we have already seen the concept of the standard of living is itself open to debate. Relative poverty is, however, a very important subject which will attract increasing attention in the future. Within LDCs, for instance, if and when absolute poverty is reduced, we can expect more and more people to demand access to resources which at the moment may be concentrated in relatively few hands. In certain of the MDCs, where it is often said that there is 'no such thing' as poverty in the absolute sense, free market economics has been observed to widen inequalities. If relative poverty is defined as anyone earning less than half the European Union average, then the number of poor in the UK increased from 5 million in 1979 to some 12 million in 1993. The Canadian economist, John Kenneth Galbraith, has claimed (in his book *The Culture of Contentment*) that in countries such as the USA and the UK, there is an economic 'underclass' of unemployed and low-paid workers. This underclass provides cheap labour for the service industries (the kitchen porters and janitors of multinational hotel chains); or they work in the manufacturing sweatshops of the unofficial economy; or they are denied any work opportunities at all and exist on increasingly restricted social security benefits. Galbraith rejects the American idea of 'trickle-down' economics, and in an interview with Will Hutton of *The Guardian* he has suggested that it can be likened to feeding more oats to the horse in the hope that a few more grains will be left for those who pick scraps from the manure.

Such observations reinforce the view that 'development' is a phenomenon that can be studied wherever it occurs, and is not tied down to a geographical area of the world.

If Galbraith's idea of an 'underclass' has any validity, then in the context of development economics it suggests that there is no room for complacency in the MDCs. Economic growth is already under attack from the environmentalists who argue that it is unsustainable if it destroys the resources upon which it depends. Economic growth might, in itself, be sufficient to ensure that income levels increase, thus reducing absolute poverty, but further action is required if income is to become more evenly distributed, thus reducing relative poverty.

Income and Wealth

There are several causes of income inequality. One of these is the fact that wealth is unevenly distributed. As economists, we should be clear as to the distinction between income and wealth. Income (the reward to a factor service) can take the form of wages, rent, interest or profit. It is a *flow* variable, which means that it is measured over a period of time. Wealth, on the other hand, is a *stock* variable, and measures the market value of assets owned by an individual, household, firm or nation at a point in time. Part of this stock of wealth can be described as 'capital' to be used in the production of further wealth.

Wealth and income are related, in two ways. Firstly, flows of income can be used to create a stock of wealth. Thus a country's stock of wealth represents accumulated savings made out of the income of previous generations. Secondly, wealth can be used to generate further income. In the LDCs, for example, land ownership is very unequal, and landowners tend to have both more wealth and income than other sections of society.

Wealth can come in the form of 'tangible' assets, such as land and buildings, or it can be 'intangible', in the form of skills, abilities, and educational qualifications. In LDCs, therefore, where there are severe skill shortages, the incomes of, say, doctors, scientists, lawyers, engineers, educators can be even higher in relation to the rest of the population than they are in MDCs.

Inequalities in income and wealth might exist for long-established historical reasons, and might be perpetuated by social structure based on religion, class, caste, sex, or tradition. Economists, as economists, might not have much to say about the desirability or otherwise of such non-economic social and cultural factors; but they certainly can spill over into the economic sphere by causing what economists call 'factor immobility', or by creating 'monopoly power'. Where, for example, women are excluded from the workforce, or where the ownership of a vital resource such as oil is concentrated in the hands of a few wealthy families, then the results are not just social or political, but also economic.

As suggested earlier, government action can serve to reduce income inequalities. Progressive taxation, whereby both the level of taxation and the percentage rate of taxation increases with income has an automatic redistributive effect, especially in countries where there is a substantial 'social wage' in the form of 'free' government services. If, for instance, medical care is provided free of charge at the point of use, and is financed through a progressive system of tax, then in effect, this is a redistribution of resources from the better off to the less well off.

Changes in the size and structure of the population can have a profound effect on relative income levels. If there is a change in the number of young or old people in a country relative to the size of the population of working age, then it can be very difficult to predict whether a reduction in inequality within any given age group can or will be reflected by an overall increase in equality. It is quite possible to find that one age group will on average become worse off while another improves its position.

FIGURE 4.1
World Income Distribution: World Lorenz Curve, 1990

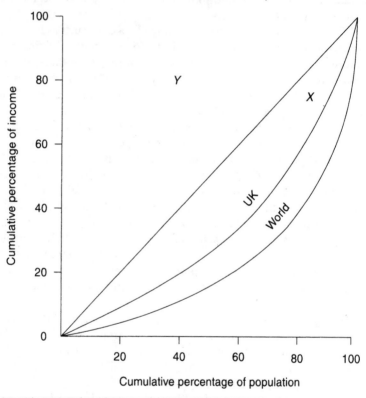

Cumulative percentage of population

Source   UNDP, *Human Development Report*, 1992.

How can we Measure Income Inequality?

A *Lorenz curve* plots the percentage of income recipients (ranked from poorest to richest) against the cumulative percentage of total income. The particular curve in Figure 4.1 ranks world population from poorest to richest. The straight line diagonal represents an equal distribution of income: along this path the poorest 20 per cent (or quintile) of people would receive 20 per cent of total income; the poorest 50 per cent would receive 50 per cent of total income, and so on. In actual fact, incomes are unevenly distributed, as shown by the Lorenz curve. The ratio between the areas X and Y on the diagram is known as the Gini Coefficient, G, where $G = X/Y$. If this is 0, then the Lorenz curve is a diagonal, and incomes are evenly distributed. The top right-hand end of the Lorenz curve always touches the top right-hand corner of the graph, as 100 per cent of the population must logically receive 100 per cent of income; but the bottom left-hand end can move away horizontally from the origin, as it is possible for a certain percentage of the population to receive no income. If the majority of the population received nothing, and just one person received everything, then the starting point of the Lorenz Curve would be almost at the bottom right-hand corner of the graph, and areas X and Y would be similar so that G would be nearly 1; similarly, the larger the 'bulge' in the curve the nearer G will be to one. It should be clear that the larger the value of G, the greater the inequality, and G cannot be greater than 1.

The UK has an uneven distribution of income, because the poorest 20 per cent of the population have only 5.8 per cent of income, while the richest 20 per cent have 39.5 per cent of income. Income in Zambia is even more unevenly distributed, however, since all the figures for the four lower quintiles are lower than the UK's. Does this mean that MDCs tend to have a more equal distribution of income than LDCs, or that that higher overall income levels will reduce inequality? Not necessarily, since countries with higher incomes than the UK (France and the USA for instance) can have a less equal distribution of income.

As well as making international comparisons at a point in time, in order to attempt an answer to the question of whether development reduces inequality, it is also necessary to make single-country comparisons over a length of time. Here, the results might still be ambiguous, as in one country the fruits of growth might accrue to one group such as the entrepreneurs or landowners, whereas in another they might be more generally spread; and we can expect social, cultural and political factors (such as the degree of democratisation) to have an effect. As we have seen, the World Bank has concluded that growth reduces poverty if two crucial conditions are met: firstly, if 'appropriate technology' is used; secondly, social services must be directed towards the poor in order to increase their productivity.

FIGURE 4.2
World Income Distribution: Income Disparity over Time

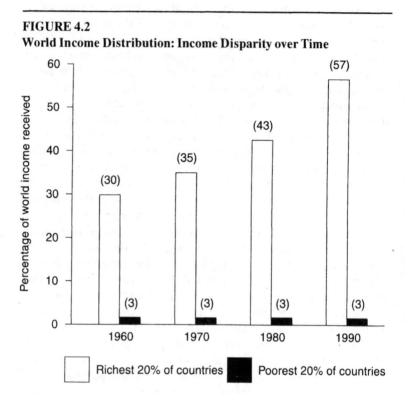

SOURCE   UNDP, *Human Development Report*, 1992.

Responsibility for the *first* condition is largely a matter for the private sector; part of the skill of being a successful entrepreneur is to use factors of production in an appropriate way.

The *second* condition is largely a function of government; the provision of a social 'safety net' is not widely regarded as the responsibility of the private sector, and most economists would doubt whether the market could be relied upon to provide one.

If both absolute and relative poverty are to be allieviated then further conditions have to be met. Governments need to consider the 'equity' or 'fairness' of their taxation systems, for example; and it is necessary to consider the role of organised labour in ensuring that those whose only asset is their muscle or brain power are properly rewarded. Perhaps an important moral to be drawn from observation of trends in the established MDCs, the existing LDCs, and the current experience of the former planned economies of Eastern Europe is that while 'markets' might stimulate *growth*, they cannot, by themselves, deliver *development*.

Why do Poorer Countries seem Prone to Disaster?

In the mid 1980s a famous television news broadcast from Ethiopia showing pictures of starving children led to a huge charity effort known as Live Aid. This event highlighted a paradox of the modern world. How is it that we in the MDCs are clever enough to transmit instant pictures of starving people from one part of the world to another, but lack the ability to instantly transmit surplus food in the other direction? Strangely, we are able to use the immutable laws of physics to our own advantage as far as telecommunications are concerned; but in the realms of food production and distribution we are slaves to the less precise man-made 'laws' of economics.

Some people believe that there is nothing that can be done about hunger and poverty in the LDCs, and that they are naturally prone to disasters, whether natural, such as floods or earthquakes, or manmade, such as wars. In many cases people become 'hardened' to news from these countries; the fact that 40 000 people died violent deaths in Liberia in 1992 is regarded as unremarkable, and they were hardly even mentioned in the western news media. Starvation in Somalia was given more prominence by news editors, but only temporarily, and it was not seen as something unexpected. In contrast, the deaths of thousands of people in Yugoslavia is regarded as unusual because, in the words of one television news reporter, 'these are scenes which we did not expect to see again in Europe'.

It is a geographical fact that LDCs are located in those parts of the world where rainfall is unpredictable, or in the hurricane or earthquake belts of the world. However, there are many MDCs which have inhospitable environments also. What makes different people susceptible to disaster is their economic circumstances. Buildings in the

American West are better able to withstand the effects of earthquake than buildings in the Philippines, simply because they are better structures; similarly, land in Pakistan which has not benefited from the investment necessary for drainage is less able to cope with flooding than land below sea level in the Netherlands. Even within LDCs, different people belonging to different social strata are affected differently by natural disasters. People with access to modern medicines and health care, for example, are less likely to be victims to disease than those without such access. Poverty and population pressures are inextricably linked to each other, and poverty in turn increases vulnerability. While a hostile environment can be a barrier to economic development, development itself is a key factor in taming an environment.

When an earthquake struck Cairo on 12 October 1992, several hundred people were killed. However, buildings in Cairo fall down every year killing hundreds of people without the help of an earthquake. With as many as 15 million people Cairo is one of the most densely populated cities in the world. It is built on a lake of brine, with a groundwater that has risen since the construction of the Aswan Dam. Basements regularly fill up with water. Meanwhile landlords attempt to create more living space by building extra storeys on to existing buildings.

In April 1993 the World Health Organisation (WHO) reported on another kind of accidental disaster: road deaths. It revealed that road accidents cause a death every 50 seconds and an injury every 2 seconds around the world. LDCs account for nearly two thirds of the 700 000 road deaths every year, and their rate is rising. Children under 15 years old account for 20 per cent of traffic fatalities in LDCs, a rate twice as high as in MDCs. Although the USA is the most motorised nation, it also has the best level of traffic safety. The problem in LDCs is largely attributable to poorer quality roads, lack of maintenance of vehicles, and poor driver training; but according to the WHO a large measure of blame is attributable to the lack of awareness of the dangers of driving under the influence of alcohol.

Disease and Famine

It is almost taken for granted that LDCs are more susceptible than MDCs to the effects of epidemics.

Cholera is killing tens of thousands of people every month in the LDCs. This is a water-borne disease, which is especially prevalent in areas with contaminated drinking water and poor sanitation. Epidemics have broken out in South America, Africa and the Far East, mainly in countries which cannot easily afford public health programmes.

Figure 4.3 gives projections for *new adult HIV infections* each year.

FIGURE   4.3
Projected New HIV Infections Each Year

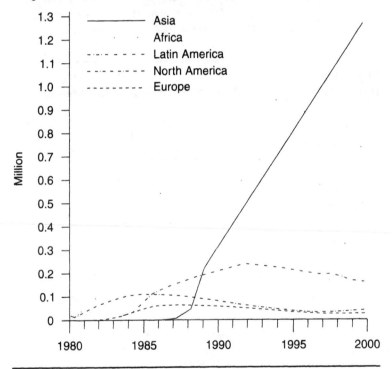

SOURCE   World Health Organisation, *Annual Report*, 1993.

Forecasts of the number of people infected in the year 2000 vary from the WHO's 40 million up to 120 million. The graph predicts that new HIV positive infections will peak in Latin America and Africa at much higher levels and much later than in the MDCs. The delay between HIV infection and developing Aids-related disease means that actual Aids cases will continue rising for decades. The most disturbing projection is for Asia, where the number of new HIV positives is expected to rise into the next century. The WHO estimates that the total worldwide cost of Aids is running at about $10 billion a year for treatment, and $80 billion through loss of earnings.

Susceptibility to disease obviously directly linked to the access which the citizens of the LDCs have to medical care, immunisation, sanitation, clean drinking water, shelter, education, and nourishment. If we focus on just one of these, food supply, we can see in Figure 4.4 that whereas the MDCs consume more than their nutritional requirements, most of the world fails to take in its daily requirement of calories.

FIGURE 4.4
Daily Calorie Supply per Head as a Percentage of Requirements

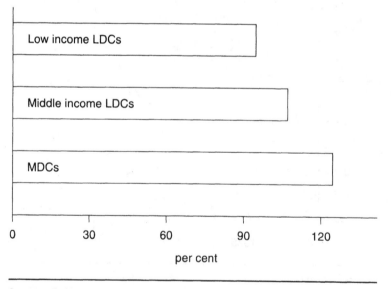

SOURCE   Oxfam, *Annual Report*, 1993.

Although the world as a whole produces enough food for everybody, roughly 780 million people (about 20 per cent of the population of LDCs) do not get enough to eat. There has been some improvement since the 1960s when the figure was over 30 per cent, but in Africa especially, very little progress has been made. There is a virtuous circle of income, health, nutrition and education. Well fed people are more likely to be healthy; health and sanitation prevent wage earners from falling ill and losing income, of which 80 per cent is spent by poor families on food. Educated women are more likely to give their children food of the right kind. Merely providing more vitamin A could prevent about 500 000 children a year from going blind. Educated women are more likely use contraceptives, thus helping to ensure that limited incomes are shared among fewer family members. Higher income per head means better health, and so the circle continues.

In April 1993 it was reported that Cuba was suffering from an epidemic linked to poor nourishment which had affected the sight of thousands of people. It was said to be an indication that the health of Cubans was affected by an economic crisis triggered by the collapse of ties with Eastern Europe and the former Soviet Union. Cuban officials claimed that shortages of vitamin-rich foods such as fresh meat, milk, eggs and bread, were made worse by a US embargo on imports which made it difficult to obtain both food and medicines.

In an article in the *Economic Review* in March 1990, B. G. Kumar of the Centre for Development Studies at Trivandrum in India, argued that whereas famines are usually thought of as happening where there is a severe reduction in the supply of food in a particular area, they can often occur where food supplies are constant or even growing. Traditional views of famine emphasise the Malthusian view of population growth outstripping food production, or a natural disaster leading to a sudden collapse of food supplies in a region or country. Kumar argues that *some* famines are explained by a decline in food availability, for instance as happened recently in Ethiopia. In Bengal, on the other hand, a famine occurred where food supply did not fall. People starved to death in front of full granaries, lacking the means by which to purchase the grain. This, he says, means that it is necessary to examine not just food availability, but also the economic forces at work: in particular, those forces that determine the distribution of incomes. The 'entitlement theory' of famines suggests that anything which disrupts a person's access to food can cause starvation. This might be a fall in that person's income, or a change in relative prices. Any change will affect different groups in different ways: landowners will be affected differently from nomadic pastoralists. For instance, a drought might kill off some of the nomads' animals, but this might not immediately cause starvation. What will be crucial is the variation in the 'exchange rate' between animals and grain. If the 'terms of trade' between oxen and grain deteriorate, then the nomads might experience a famine while the landowners do not. Kumar concludes that *laissez-faire* economics cannot be relied upon to cure famines; and neither can the policy of directly distributing food as famine relief. He suggests the possibility of improving 'exchange entitlements' with money rather than distributing food in some cases, and also the need to focus on longer term problems of designing economic systems that reduce the vulnerability of certain countries and groups within those countries to famines.

Income inequality is a man-made phenomenon, and the poor have the least resistance to natural disasters. MDCs have earthquakes, floods and epidemics, but their populations are immunised, well fed, and live in properly constructed buildings. Many Americans and Europeans live in remote and mountainous areas, but they are never too far away from emergency services, telephones, and road and rail links. Their resistance to disaster is therefore higher. Let us also remember that some disasters, such as the degradation of poorly irrigated land, and the devastation caused by military aggression, are not natural disasters at all – they are man made phenomena, and so is the inequality of incomes.

The Rural Poor and 'Empowerment'

One-fifth of the world's population are poor people living in rural areas in poor countries. According to the International Fund for Agricultural Development (IFAD) these billion people are too often regarded as people in need of charity rather than the tools to help themselves. In a report published in 1992 entitled *The State of World Rural Poverty*, the organisation claimed that while food aid and similar gifts were appropriate to emergency situations, in the long run what is really needed is to provide the poor with land, technology and credit, to allow them to fend for themselves. The rural poor would be helped, for instance, by changes in the tax policies of their governments to help redistribute incomes to the poor, by local savings groups to provide the credit that commercial banks cannot, by agricultural investment which is more concerned with growing food rather than exporting it, and by an end to discrimination when women (whose poverty is growing faster than men's) try to obtain credit or gain access to other resources.

Perhaps the most important and meaningful word in the vast amount of jargon invented by development economists is the word 'empowerment'. Essentially, this means 'helping the poor to help themselves'; and nowhere is the need for empowerment more crucial than in the role of women in the LDCs.

Poverty and the Role of Women

Perhaps it is because economics has tended to be a male-dominated profession that textbooks often concentrate on what might be seen as 'technical' issues such as interest rates and commodity prices rather than what could be termed 'human' or 'family' issues. In a world where more than 60 per cent of all households are headed by women, and where the percentage is much higher in countries where many men are forced by economic circumstances to find work as migrants, this must lead to a discussion of the role of women.

Income inequality is not a purely economic phenomenon. It is created by society's opinions of the relative importance of capital and labour, and the value it places on different kinds of labour. Similarly gender inequality is not purely a biological phenomenon. It is created by society's opinions of the relative importance of men and women. Income divisions can make huge differences to the life experiences of human beings, and so can gender divisions. The two are, in fact, closely linked.

In LDCs women traditionally undertake those tasks which tend to be the last to benefit from labour-saving devices. While men's work, such as tending the fields or irrigation, is assisted by rudimentary technology, (ploughs, pumps, etc.), the women's tasks of fetching water, cooking and rearing children tend to remain arduous and time-consuming. Drive along a road in Kenya and you will see women carrying enormous loads on their heads; as soon as some technology appears – in the form, for example, of an ox-cart constructed from an old car chassis – invariably it will be driven by a man. Economic development often actually displaces women and worsens their position. India, for example, has the largest concentration of match factories in the world. In those factories where matches are placed into matchboxes by hand, this low-paid work is done by women. In those factories where the process has been mechanised, wages are higher, but jobs are fewer, and these jobs are nearly always done by men.

The working hours of women tend to be longer than those of men. UNICEF has estimated that women produce about half the world's food. In Africa and Asia, women are estimated to be responsible for producing some 80 per cent of all agricultural products, and 60 per cent of the cash crops which earn foreign exchange. In many LDCs, men's work ends in the afternoon, when men gather in social groups for rest and recreation. Women, on the other hand, are expected to follow a day at work in the fields with many hours seeing to the rest of their family duties. While the typical man's working day might be 6 to 8 hours in the morning, followed by an afternoon of socialising with other men, women typically work 10 to 12 hours in the fields, followed by another 6 to 8 hours in their domestic and child-rearing roles.

Empowerment is a phrase which is beginning to be used by development agencies. In order for development programmes to have a 'gender perspective' which will empower women they need to consciously promote projects which raise the status of women. They can do this by educating women to have control over their own bodies, giving women access to resources, and encouraging women to organise themselves and cooperate at a grass roots level.

Development programmes fail when they treat all recipients of development as if they were the same. As well as recognising and catering for differences in gender it is also important to make allowances for the special needs of other social groups such as children, elderly people, ethnic minorities and the disabled.

Most of the women living in LDCs are in rural areas, where farming is often at subsistence level. Often, the facilities which women need to empower themselves are to be found in the cities. If, for instance, a woman has to leave the fields and her family for several days to visit a hospital, then this causes a serious dilemma, and it might not even be possible for a family to consider it; therefore programmes providing basic social facilities and health care at a local level are vital to the idea of empowerment.

In many LDCs women have few *ownership rights*; any improvements in land and buildings are likely to add to the income and wealth of men rather than women. Land reform and changes in agriculture often make women's lives worse: they might, for example, lose an independent source of income when they find that it is no longer worthwhile producing a small cash crop for sale at a market, when their prices are undercut by mass produced goods from elsewhere.

Some people see improved educational opportunities as the key to economic development, and it is often said that women are the driving force for education and socialisation within a family; and yet of the world's population who are illiterate, the majority are women. It is widely recognised that improved educational standards are an important key to development; education is an important investment activity for any LDC; what is particularly productive in terms of economic and social returns is the education of girls.

Perhaps this goes some way towards explaining why it is quite possible to find economic development having little or no effect on family sizes. In Latin America, for instance, where the Roman Catholic church is very influential, there are religious taboos on contraception; and in many LDCs where men traditionally make decisions, it would be impossible to introduce effective family planning without a complete change of attitudes about the role of women in society. Compare the Latin American experience with that of the strongly Catholic countries of Western Europe. In Spain, more liberal social attitudes towards women and the assertion by women of their rights has led to a dramatic reduction in average family sizes. This has been achieved through the increased use of contraception in spite of religious prohibitions, and has coincided with rapid economic growth and higher living standards.

The activities of multinational companies have been criticised where they have targeted women with inappropriate products. The marketing of dried milk for babies in countries with unreliable water-supplies is a case in point. As public opinion has moved towards breast-feeding in MDCs, certain multinationals have sought to open up new markets in the LDCs, and relief agencies are having to devote precious resources to educational programmes to combat the tide of misleading information from these businesses. Another educational problem arises from the attempts by tobacco companies to combat the pressures of a contracting market by selling in LDCs where government controls on tobacco advertising are weak or non-existent. Where a husband begins to divert precious family resources on an unnecessary smoking habit, or where a family eventually loses a breadwinner through a smoking-related disease, it is the woman who pays the long-term price.

The process of economic development often ignores women and bypasses them; it can even worsen their position. If women are to participate in the fruits of development then they must be freed from the tyranny of large families and subsistence survival. If all other arguments against population control fall, then this is one argument in its favour which is overwhelming.

Feeding the World

5

Why is it that luxury vegetables from Africa are on sale in supermarkets in the UK, when the media lead us to believe that there is chronic hunger in their country of origin? Why do LDCs export foodstuffs, when their own citizens are short of food? Why would a country facing starvation sell cash crops to industrialised countries? Why are some peasant farmers forced off the land in LDCs, while cereals which they could have grown themselves are imported? The majority of families in a Kenyan town do not have running water in their houses. In the distance they can see sprinklers watering fields of flowers to be sent to Europe for Mother's Day. What is going on?

Famine, Chronic Hunger and Nutrition

Since the early 1980s television and newspaper reports of famine in north-east Africa have raised consciousness and compassion among millions of people in MDCs. Famine leads to mass starvation, and is a result of an acute failure of food supply. Thankfully famines have been relatively rare in recent years, but *chronic hunger* – sustained nutritional deprivation – has been experienced by countless millions. It rarely gets the attention of the news media, but may kill more people than famine. The distinction between famine and chronic hunger is well made by the contrast between the Great Leap Forward in China in 1958–61, when 15–25 million people may have died of famine, and the chronic hunger of India which hastens the deaths of two or three million people a year. Thus, while India avoids famine, it suffers increased deaths equivalent to the Chinese famine over a period of seven or eight years. A further complication arises from the fact that the results of famine are tragically measurable, but calculations of the numbers suffering from chronic hunger in the world are beset with problems of definition. No particular medical test, income level or calorific intake can identify it. A World Bank report of 1985, using income methods, suggested that between 340 and 730 million people (between 7 and 15 per cent of world population) did not have the income to obtain enough energy from their diet.

The distressing images of famine trigger memories of apocalyptic predictions of mass starvation. Ever since Malthus predicted 'population outrunning the means of subsistence' in his *Essay on Population* in 1797, there have been attempts to link overpopulation to food supply. In the 1960s Paul Erlich's book *The Population Bomb* argued that the battle to feed humanity was already lost and that hundreds of millions would starve to death in the 1970s and 1980s. The idea of *resource depletion* was popular in the 1970s, and in 1972 the Club of Rome predicted the dates when key raw materials would run out. These included petroleum in 1992, copper and lead in 1993 and natural gas in 1994. These gloomy predictions have not come about, indeed known reserves of many minerals are now greater than in 1972. The world's food production per capita actually grew by 30 per cent between 1951 and 1992, and according to the World Bank only 11 per cent of the world's land surface was being used for agricultural crops in 1993.

The problem of feeding the world is not, therefore, caused by the earth approaching the limits of its carrying capacity, but of the organisation of human beings. Economists call this the distribution question. It is worth remembering that wars, civil wars and political upheavals bear the greatest responsibility for the famines in Ethiopia, Eritrea and Rwanda in recent years. The 1997 *World Development Report* argues that the role of the state is all important in development. Various correlations of the relationship between development and the stability of the state are attempted, and famines are seen in the context of the breakdown of the state.

If famine and hunger can be explained by maldistribution rather than lack of global food supply, why does this happen? One answer is that it results from income inequality. Consumers in MDCs can afford to pay such high prices that, for example, their purchasing power can make it worth growing and air-freighting mange-tout peas from Zambia and offering them for sale in Britain. More than fifty countries now export coffee, a favourite drink in MDCs, while it is not particularly popular in many of the exporting countries. These are examples of *cash crops*, and an important distinction must be made between cash crops and *subsistence crops*.

Subsistence crops, such as millet, coarse rice, plantains, and root crops, are grown to feed the farmer's family. No cash is generated unless there is a surplus which can be taken to market. *Cash crops*, on the other hand, might not figure in the local diet at all, and are grown almost entirely for cash. They include coffee, cocoa, tobacco, exotic fruits and vegetables, and nuts. They are usually sold through middlemen, or through government agencies; or they might be produced for huge multinational food processing companies. For this reason, they tend to come from large commercial farms rather than traditional peasant farms. Cash crops are exported in order to earn foreign exchange: hard currency which can be used by governments to finance imports of medicines, machinery, roads – in other words to develop their economies – or to buy consumer durables, or to service international debts. LDC governments are keen to foster cash cropping, but it leaves the people who work in traditional farming without the income to take part in the new 'monetised' economy.

Another reason for low incomes is *underemployment*. Unemployment is very much a feature of the developed world. Workers are free agents who are employed for productivity-related wages or are unemployed, in which case they look for work elsewhere. So work in MDCs involves time discipline and a sharp separation of remunerated work time and leisure or rest time. But in traditional rural areas of many LDCs all members of the kinship or family group work in flexible mixtures of commodity production. There may be some waged work and sharing of wages within the group. Rights to land change if people move or die. For these reasons, a traditional rural economy is characterised by underemployment rather than unemployment. People stay where they are rather than looking elsewhere for work, and this means that what work there is tends to be shared out among all members of the community. Taking people away to form an urban workforce would not necessarily lower productivity. Thus income levels per head are too low to form the sort of effective demand backed by purchasing power which drives the MDC or the modern sector of the LDC.

Terms of Trade

If the purchasing power of individuals is low, so is that of the LDC as a whole. If we compare the *prices* of a country's exports and imports on world markets (not the *quantities* being traded) we can calculate a *terms of trade index* for that country

$$\text{Terms of trade index} \quad = \quad \frac{\text{Export price index} \times 100}{\text{Import price index}}$$

The export price index measures changes in the general level of export prices, and the import price index does the same with import prices. As with all index numbers there is a starting point or base year which must be the same for both exports and imports. Multiplying exports by one hundred defines the terms of trade index as a ratio of the export price index to the import price index.

An increase in the terms of trade index number indicates a *favourable shift* or *improvement* in a country's terms of trade, and means that for a given amount of exports, more can be imported. A decrease in the terms of trade index number indicates an *adverse shift* or *deterioration* in the country's terms of trade and means that for a given quantity of imports, more will have to be exported.

It must be remembered that this only tells us about relative values, not volumes. So, whether a favourable shift in the terms of trade will improve a country's balance of trade depends on the elasticities of demand for exports and imports. The concept which relates the terms of trade to the balance of trade is the *Marshall–Lerner condition*. This states that a favourable shift in the terms of trade will improve the balance of trade only if the coefficients of demand elasticity for both imports and exports (defined as positive numbers) add up to less than 1 (that is, if the total demand for exports and imports is inelastic). An unfavourable shift in the terms of trade (caused, for example through devaluation) will improve the balance of trade if the coefficients of demand elasticity for imports and exports add up to more than one. Since the LDCs have historically tended to deal in goods which have low elasticities, it suggests that these countries tend to suffer trade deficits when their terms of trade indices deteriorate. Figure 5.1 shows the linkage between an adverse shift in the terms of trade and a tendency to trade deficits, through price inelasticity in import and export markets. A trade deficit may contribute to exchange rate depreciation, which, through dearer imports and cheaper exports, causes further deterioration in the terms of trade in a vicious circle. For comparison, the virtuous circle enjoyed by MDCs is also shown.

FIGURE 5.1
Terms of Trade, the Marshall–Lerner Condition and the Balance of Trade in LDCs and MDCs

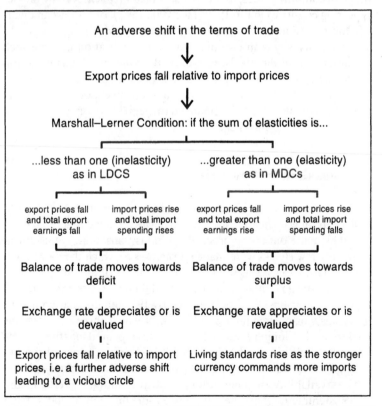

The deterioration in the terms of trade of LDCs is a constant theme of the last seventy years. The real prices (adjusted for inflation) of commodities other than oil exported by developing countries started to fall in the wake of the depression of 1929–32, fell a quarter between 1951 and 1965, almost halved during the 1980s and continues to fall in the 1990s. The prices of manufactured goods have increased in relative terms for much of the period. Thus a country which exports tea, for instance, and imports virtually everything else finds that the terms of trade have moved against it. It must export more and more tea simply to pay for the same amount of imports of everything else. Many LDCs depend on a narrow exporting base consisting of minerals, raw materials and agricultural products such as sugar, cocoa and coffee.

The LDCs have little bargaining power with the MDCs, unless they can combine forces, in the way spectacularly achieved by the oil-exporting countries in the 1970s (see Chapter 7), or if they can diversify their economies, so that they produce a wider range of goods. This explains why cash cropping and industrialisation became such an imperative in the 1960s. However, the long run deterioration in the terms of trade, leading to trade deficits meant that LDCs had little chance of paying for industrial capital from export earnings: development would have to be financed through borrowing, or through exports from the primary sector.

The Banks and the Debt Crisis

In the 1970s and 1980s banks were falling over themselves to lend to LDCs. Credit was cheap and abundant; it was assumed that repayment would be made out of the proceeds of industrialisation, but astonishingly, very few checks were made on the uses to which the money was put. In many cases it was used to build up stocks of military hardware for militaristic governments to use against their own citizens, or it supported a war against their neighbours. By 1978 the international arms trade was worth just under $20 billion, of which three quarters was sales to the developing world. Often loans disappeared into the pockets of corrupt politicians, who deposited it back in the banks of the developed world to be re-lent, part of a process known as *capital flight*.

The availability of huge amounts of international credit in the 1970s stemmed from the suspension of the US dollar's fixed exchange rate with gold in 1971, and the accumulation of banked oil dollars earned by the OPEC cartel after their quadrupling of crude prices in 1973. The oil crisis of the mid-seventies caused recession and reduced demand for credit in the MDCs, leaving private banks quite desperate to lend the balances deposited with them by oil-producing countries. Non-oil producing LDCs, facing mounting import bills and losing traditional export markets, found the overtures of the banks and their low interest rates very appealing. LDC debt grew from under $100 billion in 1970 to over $600 billion by the end of the 1970s. However as MDCs adjusted to recession with 'new right' governments in the USA and Britain, interest rates were virtually doubled to over twelve per cent in the early eighties, springing a debt servicing trap on the LDCs and bringing the threat of default and bank failure. LDC debts spiralled to over $1000 billion by 1986 as they borrowed yet more to service existing debt while receiving less and less for exports. From 1984 debt service payments actually exceeded new borrowing, resulting in the extraordinary phenomenon of net flows of money from LDCs to MDCs – from poor to rich. The debt crisis is considered in greater depth in Chapter 8.

Stabilisation and Structural Adjustment Policies

The recommended way out of the debt trap for the LDCs was to spend less (*stabilisation policies*) or earn more (*structural adjustment policies*). Spending less meant reducing imbalances in external and domestic accounts by cutting government programmes for such things as health, education, transport and infrastructure, and depressing expenditure by firms and households. Cutting government spending on merit goods such as education and health has made LDCs even less equal in their income distribution. The consequences of this deflationary approach were disastrous, and UNICEF, for instance, estimates that half a million children die every year as a result of the debt crisis and its effects on health services.

How could the LDCs earn more? The standard advice from the main international agencies, including the IMF, World Bank and the UN's Food and Agriculture Organisation (FAO) has been the *Structural Adjustment Programme*. This is covered in greater depth in Chapter 8, but its implications are that the LDCs should, in effect, liquidate their natural capital. They do this by turning their forests into timber, their fisheries into fishmeal, and their subsistence farm-lands into cash crops. The aim is to increase the supply of goods that can be traded as exports. In other words, they grow food for export, in order to earn foreign exchange. It is a long way from the hoped-for industrialisation of the 1960s.

India, for example, has a large debt ($70 billion in 1992) which, critics state, makes it a slave to the west. Advice to the Indian government on tackling this debt offered by the IMF included a Structural Adjustment Plan, which was based on some of the so-called 'supply-side policies' fashionable in the USA during the 1980s. These included outward orientation to expose domestic producers to world prices, deregulation and the relaxation of labour laws. Cheap labour is thus a constituent, though unstated, part of such plans. As long as hard currency is earned few questions are asked about how the money is raised – the issues of whether farm labourers are exploited, cash crops replace subsistence crops, or the suffering of women and children in low-paid sweatshops do not figure in the published balance sheets.

Local Producers and International Markets

Local producers are very experienced at growing food, especially when it is for their own consumption. They are not so good at dealing with the unequal relationships that arise from working for multinational food-producers. World markets for many types of food are dominated by oligopolistic producers. For example instant coffee is produced by a handful of large companies, and the greatest value added in the production process is to be found closest to final consumers, that is, in the developed world. Retailing, marketing, packaging, distribution and processing all take place in the MDCs, and only a tiny fraction of the final price is paid to the peasant producer. The economics of cash-cropping is so fragile at the local level that a small fluctuation in world market conditions can produce local disaster.

Price Fluctuations

The prices of many cash crops, like those of other commodities such as nickel and oil, are influenced by futures markets which exist in the world's financial centres. Here, dealers buy and sell options, or contracts for delivery of commodities not yet produced. The vast majority of these dealers have no wish to actually obtain real commodities; over 90 per cent of the deals are speculative, with dealers hoping to sell their options at a profit at a later date. Speculators can switch almost instantly from one commodity to another, thus 'market sentiment' produces exaggerated upward and downward price movements.

Unfortunately, the farmers in the LDCs who supply the goods cannot switch from one commodity to another at will: they are stuck with real commodities at real prices; and contrary to what is suggested in economics textbooks they find that their prices are unrelated to the costs of production. Often, a small farmer producing cocoa or coffee beans has no choice but to sell at a loss. A whole host of intermediaries add on their margins: these include the middlemen who purchase wholesale supplies of crops; multinational brand name companies; governments (which, in LDCs often raise revenue by taxing exports); and the commodity dealers. The result is that the tiny fraction of the final price paid to the producer may itself be unstable.

Social Organisation and the Size of Farms

The proposition that the introduction of cash crops displaces local food cultivation and causes hunger is supported by a number of development economists and is often to be seen in the pages of the *New Internationalist* magazine. To verify this it is helpful to know something about the nature of social organisation and the extent of the 'commoditisation' of society. For example, is production in the hands of independent peasant farmers or large landowners who pay wages to labourers? In the first case it is only really the output of farming which has become part of monetary markets: the factors of production (land, labour, tools, decision making) remain in the hands of peasant families. Cash crop price movements are threatening, especially if they are grown to pay taxes. In the second case, labour power too has become a commodity, dependent entirely on wages and therefore it is much more vulnerable. Landless wage labourers are often the first victims of famine, when wages fall and state welfare systems are unavailable. Cash crops can provide employment, but whereas the prices paid to landowners reflect world market conditions, the wages received by workers reflect local conditions. Even if world prices rise, it might not help labourers unless other parts of the economy get stronger, and wage rates are pushed up.

Another important feature of social organisation relates to the size of farms. According to the 1996 *Human Development Report*, evidence from countries as diverse as Brazil and India supports the view that small farms make more efficient use of resources. As farm size increases, the proportion of land in use falls, as does the amount of labour used per hectare. This is because small farmers face low opportunity costs of family labour but high prices for land and capital; while large commercial farmers face high wage bills and relatively lower land and capital prices. Extending the small farm with a little extra land will give proportionally larger gains in output than replacing labour with scarce capital on the large farm, which is socially inefficient. However, to achieve this change in the social efficiency of resource use, a change in the structure of land ownership would be needed, and it is large landowners who command political power and feel the strongest urge to produce cash crops.

Export cropping induces the precise opposite of the more efficient use of resources through small landholdings described above as small farmers are pushed off the land. In the Dominican Republic, for instance, families which were self sufficient, growing their own food have been dispossessed because their land was required for sugar production. Sugar is, on the face of it, an attractive cash crop; its addictive qualities have made it a vital preservative and flavour enhancer for fast food in the developed world. Thus production has developed over many years based on presumed inelastic demand. However, health awareness campaigns in the MDCs have recently caused consumers to switch to artificial sweeteners. Sugar thus has a low price elasticity of demand in the West, but probably has a negative income elasticity: it is purchased as an 'inferior good' which people switch away from as incomes rise. Supply on the other hand is relatively elastic as more parts of the world formerly dominated by subsistence farming are commoditised and commercialised.

As the supply of cash crops such as sugar has increased on world markets, their steep demand curves and volatility caused by speculative futures markets have ensured that price has occasionally plummeted in the short run and shown a long run tendency to fall. In countries like Dominica the sugar cane fields were abandoned, the sugar-mills were closed, and people who once were able to live off the land went hungry because their land had been taken for cane fields which were now empty. Meanwhile, the government had sold the land to absent landlords, and introduced new land registration acts. Without title deeds the local people were unable to offer collateral for loans to bring the fields back into productive use. Besides, the fragile mix of tradition, culture, family structure and farming expertise cannot be brought back once dislodged.

FIGURE 5.2
The Supply of, and Demand for, Sugar

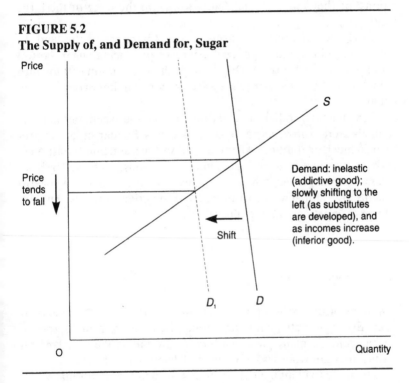

Demand: inelastic (addictive good); slowly shifting to the left (as substitutes are developed), and as incomes increase (inferior good).

Land Ownership

In many of the poorest countries people are moving out of lands which are underpopulated. They are underpopulated in the sense that they have the agricultural potential to support more people. In Brazil, for example, the richest 1 per cent of farmers own 15 times the amount of land owned by the poorest 56 per cent. Peasants are being driven into the forests because nearly all of the rest of the land has been taken over by large businesses with the help of politicians. Much of this land is not actually used for agriculture, but is held as a financial investment. Within Brazil, an area roughly the size of India lies uncultivated, while 20 million rural peasants are landless. These landless persons end up either helping to make clearings in the rainforests for farming or mining operations; or they move to the shanty towns on the edge of the large cities.

In Guatemala, just 482 farms cover 22 per cent of the land. In the Philippines, the huge agribusinesses producing sugar, cotton and pineapples for the MDCs have pushed 12 million settlers into the lowland forests, where they are obliterating important ecosystems.

In Ghana, up to half the children are malnourished, but half the land is used to grow cocoa for chocolate bars. Similar situations prevail in much of Southern Africa, South America and South East Asia, where the concentration of land into fewer hands is achieved by businesses working hand in hand with governments; often these governments are riddled with corruption, and sometimes they use military force to implement their policies.

Land Degradation

Millions of the world's population are suffering from chronic hunger. Every year 50–60 million people die early from malnutrition. Meanwhile, in many places cash crops are killing the very land on which they grow. This is known as land degradation. Peasant farmers are tempted to plant high-yield crops and abandon traditional methods where crop plants were interspersed with fruit trees providing extra food sources, giving shade and preventing soil erosion. High-yield intensive crops require full sunshine; they also need masses of fertilisers, whose prices are both cyclical and dependant on decisions made in the MDCs. Trees disappear and water sources are quickly exhausted. In the LDCs, thousands of rivers are disappearing every year.

Interdependence

MDCs are in a strong position *vis-à-vis* LDCs; they can charge more for fertilisers, seeds, and other raw materials, while paying less for the cash crops. When producers of local foodstuffs are forced off the land, local people stop investing in agriculture, and LDCs become more dependent for their foodstuffs on MDCs such as the USA and members of the EU. The giant grain-trading companies of the US and EU have a vested interest in the LDCs being unable to feed themselves: for reasons discussed below, these countries are producing huge surpluses of basic foodstuffs, and one way of disposing of these is to trade them for mangoes, chillies, runner beans, or other cash crop exports from the LDCs.

EU Surpluses

There is a conflict of interest between the consumers and producers of agricultural products. Whereas consumers wish to pay low prices for as large a quantity as possible, producers often find that their incomes fluctuate with the size of harvest. When their crop is in short supply, prices and incomes rise accordingly. This is because elasticity of demand tends to be low, so that the revenue gained from an increase in price is greater than the revenue lost from the resulting reduction in quantity demanded. The opposite is also true: a good harvest causes prices to fall but the extra quantity demanded does not compensate.

Since World War II, all Western governments have protected their farmers' incomes. Their aim has been to safeguard food supplies by offering some price stability. Critics would claim that governments have been unduly influenced by the vocal farming lobby, and by pressure from the large corporations supplying agribusinesses with yield-boosting chemicals.

Different governments have supported their agricultural sectors in different ways; in Japan, for example, rice producers are protected by quotas on imports. In the EU, a system of intervention purchasing has been used.

The idea behind the Common Agricultural Policy (CAP) of the EU is that the authorities would act as a 'swing' consumer and supplier. In years of good harvests, the authorities would add to demand by purchasing surpluses, thus shifting the demand curve to the right, and increasing price to the floor level. During years of bad harvests, the authorities would release stocks, shifting the supply curve to the right, and stabilising prices, as in Figure 5.3.

FIGURE 5.3
Price Stabilisation through Buffer Stocks

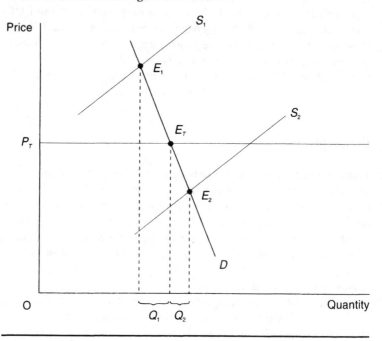

KEY

D = Demand curve (assumed to be stable)
P_T = Target price
E_T = Target equilibrium
S_1 = Supply during 'bad' harvest
E_1 = Equilibrium when supply is low
S_2 = Supply during 'good' harvest
E_2 = Equilibrium when supply is high
Q_1 = Quantity released from stock after 'bad' harvest
Q_2 = Quantity added to stock after 'good' harvest

However, in practice, surpluses have become more or less permanent. Producers have had a vested interest in achieving over-production,
and the result has been mountains of grain, butter and meat, and
lakes of milk and wine. Over time, the supply curve shifts to the right
as the productivity of agriculture improves with better crops and
technology, causing intervention purchasing to grow. Attempts to
reduce intervention prices are often met with vocal opposition from
the farmers. This has had a debilitating effect on the EU itself, which
has had to spend taxpayer's money on maintaining and disposing of
its surpluses.

Protectionist policies like the CAP affect LDCs in several ways.
They encourage the further production of certain cash crops. Surplus
dairy products are produced by giving European cattle soya feed
grown in LDCs. Then, when surplus dairy products go on the market
they depress world prices. This undermines local markets, and LDC
farmers lose their livelihood.

If some of the EU surplus is dumped on to markets in the LDCs,
farmers in those countries cannot compete with the subsidised prices.
Even if local farmers are efficient enough to compete with EU farmers,
they are certainly not efficient enough to compete with the Treasur-
ies of EU governments.

The CAP also acts as a barrier to exports from the LDCs. For
example, whereas the UK can import coal from South Africa or Australia because it is cheaper than UK coal, it cannot import meat or
grain from LDCs because subsidy renders European agricultural
products artificially competitive. The Uruguay Round of the GATT
talks stalled during 1992 because of the insistence of LDCs, together with the USA, that the CAP should cease to be a barrier to
trade.

Alternatives to Cash Crops

How can LDCs break out of the tyranny of debt-repayments and cash
crops? Some are relying on a crop whose price is predicted to increase steadily over the next ten years in response to growing world
demand. While there has been a decline in consumption and a harsher regulatory climate in certain of the MDCs, 40 per cent of the market is in the newly-deregulated markets of the former planned
economies. This crop is tobacco. The LDCs themselves are also a

potential market for the multinational enterprises (MNEs) which manufacture tobacco products (See Figure 5.4).

According to medical opinion, the output of the tobacco multinationals kills a sizeable proportion of their market each year, while passive smoking harms innocent bystanders. According to economists, tobacco products contain *negative consumption externalities*, that is, costs which are not in the price but which are borne by whoever pays for the failing health of the smoker. While a packet of 20 cigarettes costs the equivalent of $4.50 in Britain of which just over 80 per cent is tax, it is only $1.93 in the USA of which 29 per cent is tax (at August 1997). While it could be argued that some of the cost of treating the 35 000 lung cancer sufferers in Britain is paid by smokers, in the USA the healthcare bill is less well covered. Taxes on cigarettes yield about $13 billion dollars a year in both countries, though the American market is much bigger. For this reason a deal worth $368 billion was negotiated in June 1997 between 40 states of the USA and all the big tobacco companies, allowing healthcare authorities to recover costs associated with smoking.

This remarkable *internalisation* of an *externality* seems bound to set the precedent for similar agreements in Britain. But the settlement in the USA has fewer implications in the LDCs. For example, in Vietnam the 72 million population is growing at two per cent a year, half the population is under 25, and 72 per cent of Vietnamese men are smokers. On demographics alone, there are large opportunities for the tobacco companies, two of whom, Philip Morris and British American Tobacco, have their products made under licence by the state tobacco monopoly. Countries like Vietnam and India (100 billion cigarettes a year) are not as litigious as the MDCs, so there is plenty of room for the expansion of this particular cash crop.

It is a cause for concern that from the producers' point of view the LDCs are seen as a reservoir of new customers. In fact, most tobacco consumption takes place in tobacco-growing countries. Cigarette consumption may be in long term decline in the USA and western Europe, but tobacco company advertising can continue to portray smoking as a fashionable habit in the LDCs. (See Figure 5.4.) Visitors to LDCs are often astonished to find that a population with many of its members at starvation levels are surrounded by advertisements for western gimmicks. The corporations which produce them understand only too well the psychology which allows people without

FIGURE 5.4
Tobacco: Forecast Sales in MDCs and LDCs

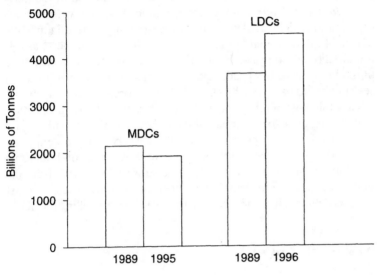

Sᴏᴜʀᴄᴇ World Health Organisation, *Annual Report*, 1993.

the basics of life to be willing to spend whatever little money they have on their products.

What can the MDCs Do?

There would seem to be some doubt as to whether international trade is benefiting all countries involved, as suggested by economic theory, or whether it is benefiting only the richer countries involved in the international trading system. World trade is currently under re-negotiation, both in Europe, with a reform of the CAP, and in the wider world, as the recommendations of the GATT Uruguay Round are implemented. (See Chapter 7.) There is a danger that reforms might actually make matters worse for the LDCs, by opening them up to a flood of cheap grain exports from the MDCs, thus depressing local market prices.

Consumers purchasing goods from the LDCs can improve their awareness of physical conditions in the countries of origin of the food that they eat. There is no shortage of information these days (*The Green Consumer Guide*, for example, together with various organisations dedicated to 'ethical investment'). The oligopolistic nature of international food suppliers is actually a help here, as it is not too difficult to research the origins of foodstuffs when each type of food only has a few producers. Thus consumers can, for instance, seek out brand names such as Café Direct, an organisation which cuts out a whole host of middlemen and directs a much larger proportion of its selling price to the actual food producers on the ground.

The mania for cash crops is related to debt servicing problems, and it is worth noting that in relation to bank assets the total amounts owed are relatively small: and banks also receive tax relief on any sums they set aside for bad debts. In certain circumstances the most beneficial policy all round would be that of simply cancelling the debts.

What can the LDCs Do?

Trickle-down economics is being seriously questioned in the MDCs. The USA, for example, supplies over 60 per cent of the total world supply of wheat. Few people actually work the land and money goes into research, new hybrid seeds, fertiliser, and machine technology. Farms have had to get larger and larger to survive. But the wealth created by the larger farmers has not trickled down to the smaller ones, who have gone bankrupt. In the US, with a lot of fertile land and relatively few agricultural workers, industries have absorbed the displaced workers. In the LDCs food production is far more labour-intensive, and there is less industry to soak up the newly unemployed. It has been argued that a 'bottom up' approach is more appropriate than 'trickle down', and that investment should be directed primarily at the poor farmer.

It is often argued that voluntary agencies like CAFOD, OXFAM or Christian Aid are better placed than the official agencies to direct aid and assistance. Their emphasis is on small-scale projects which aim at making labour more productive, rather than replacing it with machinery or promoting dependence on expensive fertilisers. This is complemented by farmers' cooperatives and trying to sell their product direct, cutting out middlemen.

Industrialisation: The Key to Development?

Is industrialisation the key to development? Is it logically possible or desirable in practice for all countries to become exporting manufacturing countries?

Whereas most LDCs regard industrialisation as a central objective of their development policy, it has been criticised for widening the gap between rich and poor, and for increasing external costs such as those caused by pollution. However, it would be unusual to find the government of an LDC committing itself to no industrial growth at all. What is crucial is the kind of industry adopted, and the issue of whether industry can prosper without causing the decline of the countryside.

The Historical Background

Industrialisation has transformed the world since the beginning of the nineteenth century in such a way that it is not just a means of development but a virtual imperative for those countries which have not yet embarked on it. The first countries to do so – Britain, the United States and Germany – did so with their own capital, relatively little foreign borrowing, and the purchasing power of their own home or imperial markets. As a result their growth rates were (and remain) relatively slow. In the twentieth century, global capital markets and imported technical knowledge have enabled the second generation of industrial powers, such as Japan, to maintain much faster growth rates. Thus the high living standards enjoyed by Britain and Japan today are a product of two hundred years of growth at a long run rate of about two per cent for Britain and about ninety years at about five per cent for Japan. The latest countries to industrialise seem to have even higher growth rates: the recent fall to eight per cent growth was a matter for concerned discussion in Singapore.

The result of this is that the lead established by the older industrial powers has been rapidly eroded, with an ever widening gap between the income levels of *all* the MDCs and the LDCs.

Stage Theories of Development

W. W. Rostow, an American professor of economic history, has suggested in his book *The Stages of Economic Growth* that societies pass through five stages of economic growth. These are summarised in Box 6.1. Firstly, in the *traditional society*, people stick to age-old customs and traditions, and the allocation of resources is largely determined by ancient traditions. Output per head is low, and does not change much from year to year. Secondly comes a stage where *preconditions for take-off* are established; the traditional economic systems become largely ceremonial and have little impact on the workings of the economy, or they are thrown off altogether. Capital is accumulated by a saving class. The economy becomes more open to modern technology. Thirdly at the *take-off* stage, any remaining barriers to growth are overcome, and growth becomes the normal condition of at least one sector ('the leading sector') of the economy. Growth begins to feed upon itself and becomes self sustaining, because the economy is able to generate its own new investment from the earnings of previous investments. Fourthly, in the *drive to maturity*, the economy diversifies (new industries are developed, beyond those which triggered the take-off), there is less reliance on imports, and more exports are produced and sold. Eventually, there arrives an age of *mass consumption*, when an affluent population consumes sophisticated durable goods and the service sector becomes a major part of the economy. Each stage is linear and is not repeated.

BOX 6.1

A Model of Economic Growth, W. W. Rostow, 1960

Stage 1: Traditional Society
- Stagnant and static society, with subsistence agriculture dominating, some craft industries
- strong social stratification

Stage 2: Preconditions for Take-off
- change primarily through external forces
- development of roads and railways
- growing exports (mining and cash-cropping)
- new social and political elite

Stage 3: Take-off
- occurs when investment increases beyond 10% of GNP
- one or two manufacturing sectors with high rates of growth
- political, social and institutional change favouring dynamic growth

BOX 6.1 *(contd.)*

Stage 4: Drive to Maturity
- self-sustaining growth
- impact of growth spreads to all areas and all sectors of economy
- decreasing social inequality

Stage 5: High Mass Consumption
- shift in sectoral dominance to durable consumer industries (cars, washing machines, etc)
- growth of service sector
- welfare capitalism(?)

Stage theories of economic development are not new. Karl Marx's analysis of the evolution of society from feudalism to capitalism to communism was itself typical of interpretations suggested by early nineteenth century German economists. Rostow's ideas were proposed as a 'Non-Communist Manifesto' in 1960, in the cold war battle for the loyalty of the Third World.

If Rostow's thesis is accepted, it suggests important lessons for policy-makers in MDCs. If aid is given and Foreign Direct Investment (FDI) is encouraged for LDCs at the take-off stage, the process of development can be accelerated. It is no longer necessary to wait for capital accumulation and for capital markets to form, as the savings and institutions of the MDCs can be used. Also, the LDC is encouraged to identify its leading sector (perhaps textiles or transport infrastructure) and to consider its relationship with the traditional sectors such as agriculture.

Development economists have tended to be critical of Rostow's theory, mainly because it is written in very general terms. Rostow is vague about exactly what factors are responsible for take-off, and it is difficult to empirically test the theory, since policy-makers within a given country are unable to tell exactly what 'stage' has been reached: in reality, stages merge into each other. However, Rostow does have the merit of drawing attention to the role of long-term investment, which is something that politicians, whose horizons are based on short-term electoral considerations, tend to forget. He also reminds us about the importance of political and sociological preconditions for development – issues which economists tend to ignore because of the difficulty of measuring the social costs of an economic upheaval.

Structural Change: Fisher–Clark Theory

A simpler stage theory is the sectoral change thesis put forward by the economists Fisher and Clark. The Fisher–Clark theory makes the distinction between three stages of production – primary, secondary and tertiary. *Primary production*, typically agriculture, is dominant in low income LDCs such as those shown in Table 6.1, but the primary sector also includes other activities associated with the factor of production land, such as fishing, mining, quarrying and forestry. *Secondary production* consists of industrial production including manufacturing and construction, and this sector looms large in middle-income economies. Lastly the *tertiary sector*, includes all services such as tourism, healthcare and education. The service sector's dominance is seen as a sign of maturity in the development process, contributing over two thirds of value added in high-income economies.

TABLE 6.1
Sectoral Balance of Selected Countries:
Percentage Distribution of Value Added in Agriculture,
Industry and Services in 1995, or most recent year available.
GNP per capita per year in US Dollars

	GNP p.c.	*Agriculture*	*Industry*	*Services*
Low Income				
Tanzania	120	**58**	17	24
Georgia	440	**67**	22	11
Albania	670	**56**	21	23
Middle Income				
Indonesia	980	17	**42**	41
Romania	1 480	21	**40**	39
Brazil	3 640	14	**37**	49
High Income				
United Kingdom	18 700	2	32	**66**
United States	26 980	2	26	**72**
Denmark	29 890	4	29	**67**

SOURCE   *World Development Report*, 1997.

The distinction between the sectors is not as clear-cut as implied above. A television set for example, is a product of all three sectors: from the extraction of oil and ores; to manufacturing, where plastics and metals are turned into an assembled final product; to the service sector where the good is transported, retailed, advertised, insured and so on. In Table 6.1, differences in the sectoral balance between groups of low, middle and high income countries are illustrated clearly.

Countries are assumed to pass from dependence on primary to secondary to tertiary sector activity as development proceeds. It is quite possible that an LDC with a large government bureaucracy and reliant for its standard of living on tourism could have a large tertiary sector without in any real sense having what could be described as a 'mature' economy. Neither should it necessarily be assumed that a large tertiary sector can be used to define an MDC. Japan and Germany, for example, have retained larger secondary sectors for longer than many other MDCs, yet both countries also have the full range of income-elastic services associated with high-income economies. In the UK, a strong body of opinion now holds the view that an over-reliance on service industries is a mistake, and that it is possible for the manufacturing base to become too small. Similarly, it is not necessarily the case that agriculture should automatically be associated with LDCs. New Zealand, a high-income country, has retained a large agricultural sector. These examples of apparent slight departures from Fisher–Clark reflect the overlaying influence of comparative advantage.

As can be seen from Table 6.1, empirical evidence supports the Fisher–Clark pattern, and it has some theoretical underpinning as well, particularly in the case of the shift from agriculture to industry. Economists are familiar with an idea known as *Engel's Law*, which states that as incomes increase, a declining proportion of income is spent on food. This, it is often said, is because of the 'fixed capacity' of the human stomach. A person earning, say $100 per year might find it necessary for survival to spend all of that income on food, but it would be physically impossible for a person earning $100 000 to purchase and consume the food represented by even half of that income. Food is therefore *income inelastic*. Furthermore, certain basic foodstuffs are purchased as *inferior goods*, which means that their income elasticities are negative. Thus, as incomes increase people to some extent switch away from such basic items as rice, bread and potatoes and substitute them with higher protein foodstuffs; and as their incomes rise still further total expenditure on food increases, but food takes a declining proportion of household income.

As industrialisation boosts incomes and agricultural productivity improves through mechanisation, movement away from agriculture takes place. In a very poor country, a very large proportion of income is spent on food: in an extreme example of a subsistence economy the proportion might be very high indeed. As incomes rise, the amount of money spent on food might increase, but expenditure on food as a percentage of total expenditure can be expected to fall, as consumers purchase other items such as manufactured consumer goods as well. This, together with the massive productivity increases brought about by improved farming technology means that a country like the UK can feed its population while only 2 per cent of its workforce is involved in agriculture. In high-income countries generally 5 per cent of the workforce was engaged in agriculture in 1990, compared with 32 per cent in middle income countries and 69 per cent in low-income countries. In Latin America and sub-Saharan Africa as much as 70 per cent of consumer expenditure is on food.

Economic development is therefore likely to be accompanied by the migration of labour from rural to urban areas.

The Dual-sector Development Model

Theories of structural change can give the impression that LDCs have economies that are closely identified with a narrow range of activities. In practice, the economies of LDCs can be surprisingly complex when one scratches the surface. To the casual visitor, such as the tourist, an LDC might seem to be dominated by traditional farming and folk crafts, but often there is a thriving (but perhaps relatively small) commercial sector existing alongside. A model of economic development suggested by Sir Arthur Lewis in 1954 investigates the main features of these 'dual economies'. The assumptions of the Lewis model are that:

1. A dual economy consists of a traditional sector and a modern sector.
2. The traditional sector consists mainly of agriculture, largely at the subsistence level. There is low productivity, low investment in capital, and surplus labour.

3. The modern sector has industrial activity such as mining, plantations and food processing. The working population exhibits rising productivity and lives in a largely urban environment. There
   is a high level of investment, much of which comes from plough-
   ed-back profits. The demand for labour is rising.

The Lewis model attempts to find a way out of the 'development
trap', where low savings lead to low investment, which leads to low
incomes, and in turn leads to low savings. His aim was to explain
the process by which a country which was previously saving less
than 5 per cent of its national income becomes an economy where
the 'average propensity to consume' is more than 15 per cent. Lewis
pointed out that the propensity to save of people on low incomes is
lower than that of people on higher incomes; he therefore suggested that a general increase in incomes would tend to be spent
on consumer goods rather than on investment. He concluded
that the expansion of a modern capitalist sector was a necessary
precondition for development; incomes would be concentrated
among the few, but this would lead to relatively high savings and
therefore high investment. Lewis was not centrally concerned about
whether this capitalist sector was owned by private sector entrepreneurs, or whether it was ultimately controlled by the state; but
in this model we have a theoretical underpinning for some of the
ideas of 'trickle-down economics' advocated by many free-market
economists in the 1980s.

Lewis focuses on the idea of there being a surplus of labour in the
traditional sector, together with a rising demand for labour in the
modern sector. He argues that much of the labour being used on the
land is in fact *disguised unemployment* as it is not being used product-
ively. (This is analogous to the idea of underemployment considered
in Chapter 5.) In effect, the traditional sector provides the modern
sector with an unlimited labour supply, at a wage rate greater than
the average product of labour in the subsistence sector by just enough
to lure workers to leave their traditional way of life. When the labour
surplus has been eliminated, the LDC is transformed into a modern
economy, with general living standards well above the subsistence
level.

The basic message conveyed by the Lewis model is that workers
can be transferred from rural to urban occupations without a country
losing output of food. Because rural productivity is so low, a person

leaving the countryside would have little or no impact on food production in the village left behind. The village would produce the same amount of food but consume less. With the income earned in the factory this person could now purchase the surplus food which had been left behind.

In the traditional sector, where food is produced for the household's own consumption, and everyone has a place at the family table, the worker's income is the share of family output, that is, the average (not the marginal) output of the family. It is therefore quite possible that in the rural areas many workers have a zero or even negative marginal output. That is to say an additional worker or family member might add nothing to total family income (zero marginal product), or might even prove to be a burden, reducing the capacity of the family as a whole to produce food, and therefore actually reducing total family income (negative marginal product).

FIGURE 6.1
The Lewis Model

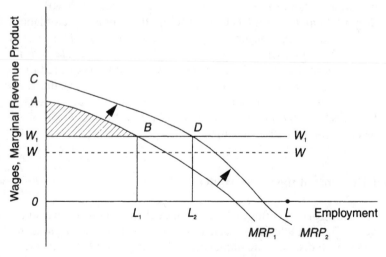

In the diagram MRP is marginal revenue product (the revenue that would be received if the family's output were sold). The law of diminishing returns predicts that if all other inputs such as land and equipment are constant, then in the short run MRP will diminish. W is the subsistence wage level, W_1 is the modern wage level, the difference between W and W_1 representing a 'premium' which has to be offered to rural workers to overcome the costs of migrating to urban areas. The distance OL represents the total quantity of labour available. Employers in the modern sector take on workers up to the point where the wage rate is equal to the MRP. This gives OL_1 workers employed in the modern sector, while L_1L work in the traditional sector. It can be seen quite clearly that the MRP of workers represented by L_1L is lower than that of those workers represented by OL_1.

In the diagram the wage bill of the modern sector is represented by the area OW_1BL_1, while its revenue is $OABL_1$. This gives a surplus or profit equal to the shaded area W_1AB which is available for ploughing back into investment. Provided that capitalists choose to do this rather than spending or saving abroad, this re-investment will increase the size of the modern sector and its demand for labour, and MRP_1 will shift to MRP_2. Employment increases to L_2 and the profit available for further investment increases to W_1CD. This process will continue as long as there is disguised unemployment in the traditional sector, and therefore workers with a zero or negative MRP. Once disguised employment has been used up, the supply price of labour will rise and will no longer be represented by a horizontal line, but by a line which slopes upwards from left to right. Here, the rate of profit will begin to decline and higher wages will need to be offered to attract workers away from competing uses. Thus, while in the short term improvements in real incomes are confined to the owners of businesses, in the longer term there will be a 'trickle-down' phase where incomes are redistributed to workers.

Criticisms of the Lewis Model

A number of objections to the Lewis model have been raised over the years. For example, it has been argued that there is a strong seasonal element to disguised unemployment. It might well be that at certain times of year farm labourers are under-used; but during planting, weeding and harvesting seasons, work might well be intense; the result is that whereas MRP might be zero or negative at certain times, over the course of a year it might be positive. Secondly, it assumes that growth and development is a largely urban phenomenon, while rural areas are by their very nature less developed and suppliers of cheap labour. In practice, however, urban unemployment is common in LDCs. This is partly due to the tendency of capitalists to invest in labour-saving technology, so that a shift in the MRP line might not occur symmetrically, as it does in the diagram. The new MRP line might have a steeper gradient, thus enabling employers to achieve a higher output from their existing workforce, rather than taking on more workers (capital deepening rather than capital widening). The idea of a 'trickle-down' phase is also open to serious challenge: it might well be that entrepreneurs will decide to reduce the amount of reinvestment that takes place, and spend their money on conspicuous consumption goods instead. Even if entrepreneurs take a more socially enlightened attitude than this, there is no guarantee that it will be easy in the first place to create an entrepreneurial class in an LDC. Lewis tends to ignore the importance of investment in human capital through education and training. Without an indigenous supply of entrepreneurs, an LDC might have to rely on the importing of such skills through multinational enterprises. These corporations might well decide to repatriate any profits made rather than invest them locally.

Perhaps the most important criticism of the Lewis model is that it simply fails to fit the facts. The movement from rural areas to urban areas has actually been greater than that predicted by Lewis, and it has been greater than the rate of job-creation in industry. Wage differentials with rural areas have also been greater than predicted, while investment has had to become diverted from industry to social welfare in order to try to cope with the urban population explosion. Thus, in the face of an urban surplus of labour, the idea that disguised unemployment in the rural areas could present a strategy for development, with a smooth transfer from the villages to the cities in response to job opportunities, has proved to be over-optimistic.

The Myrdal Theory

The Swedish economist Gynnar Myrdal argued that far from developments in the modern sector proving beneficial to the traditional sector, in practice new industries might have a *harmful* effect on traditional activities such as basket-weaving and pottery-making, so that rural craft workers find that they have to compete with mass-produced goods. Instead of income trickling down to the rural areas there is instead a 'backwash' effect, with income sucked into the growth areas at the expense of the rural areas. Myrdal proposed that resources should be devoted to rural development rather than encouraging investment in urban areas.

A possible criticism of both Lewis and Myrdal is that neither adequately analyse the *motives* of the individual for moving to the urban areas. If the person whose unemployment is 'disguised' does not perceive that he or she is unemployed, then why should he or she move to the city, unless tempted by substantially higher wages? The fact is that between 1950 and 1975 some 350 million people around the world migrated in this way, so that whereas only a quarter of LDC inhabitants were urban in 1965, by the year 2010 they are expected to represent more than 50 per cent of the population of LDCs. Is it feasible that such a massive shift can be explained by the attractions of a wage rate only slightly above rural subsistence levels?

The Todaro Model

Michael Todaro has suggested that an economically rational rural labourer would migrate to an urban area if the expected lifetime earnings in the city exceeded potential rural earnings by an amount greater than the costs of moving. The Todaro model also took into account certain risks, such as the possibility of finding oneself not employed in the 'modern' sector at all, but in the murky informal sector of running errands, pulling rickshaws, shining shoes, or other urban forms of partial unemployment. Todaro's model has, in turn, been criticised by economists who suggest that far from being a risk factor, the informal economy is actually an incentive for migration. Often this sector provides about 50 per cent of all urban jobs, and it is known that many urban workers voluntarily leave the formal sector to work in the informal sector. In addition to menial jobs it also includes an incalculable number of small workshops and should be regarded as being just as 'productive' as the formal modern sector. Even those workers trapped in the menial occupations might believe that their life expectations within the infrastructure of a city are higher than they would be in a 'backward' rural area; or they might not believe this, but nevertheless find themselves trapped in the urban environment.

The Role of Government

If industrialisation is seen as a process which necessarily involves movements between two sectors, rural and urban, then as far as policy implications are concerned, two sets of issues must be identified.

First, what are the needs of those who migrate? Research suggests that migrants tend to be younger people, with family back in the rural areas, on farms to which they could return. While they have better pay than they left behind, they tend to be lower paid than established city-dwellers. What they need is education and training together with programmes to improve productivity and incomes in the informal sector. Methods need to be found, for example, to legalise work taking place in underground 'sweatshops'; the disadvantages to the informal entrepreneur of beginning to pay tax and adopting safe working practices being balanced by advantages such as access to capital at reasonable rates of interest.

Second, what are the needs of the people left behind? There is a need to make rural areas more attractive, to offset the pull of the cities. This involves addressing such issues as land ownership and tenure, and community development schemes so that villages can benefit from projects such as schools, clinics, water-wells and roads. If there is underemployment in the rural areas, then finding a pool of labour in order to construct such projects should be no problem. What is a problem is finding the finance; and this finance includes not only the 'once and for all' set-up costs, but also the recurring current costs of running such schemes. In some cases, projects can be self-financing, such as when an irrigation scheme creates enough new crops to pay for itself; but usually community schemes require at least some injection of capital, either from the national government or from an international agency. The general role of government in the development process is further discussed in Chapter 9.

Rural versus Urban: A False Dichotomy?

Today, development economists are less likely than before to see distinctions between urban and rural areas as being particularly useful guides for government policy, and they are less likely to view industry and agriculture as representing competing sectors. Instead, they are more likely to view them as complementary sectors which need to be developed in partnership. The supporters of the idea of 'appropriate technology' would claim that their recommendations are just as important for rural areas as they are for urban development – if that development is to be sustainable in the long run.

Appropriate Technology

The word 'technology' is difficult to define, but it is linked to the idea of applied science; that is, the use of human scientific knowledge to produce goods and services. It is more than applied science, however, because technology in its broadest sense has economic, social, and even cultural and artistic purposes. Consider Brunel's railway bridges and tunnels as examples of Victorian technology: they use applied science to produce artefacts which fulfil the basic function of providing a link in a transport system (hence increasing economic efficiency and providing income and employment); but they also provide wider benefits, such as bringing communities closer together – and, incidentally, enhancing the environment by looking aesthetically pleasing to the beholder. Technology can sometimes be ahead of science: it is possible for a technology to work without its designer knowing precisely why. Primitive technologies, such as craft skills, can in this sense be almost totally non-scientific.

Some modern technologies such as genetic engineering are based upon scientific principles which are often studied in a pure form before a social use is found for them, and indeed before society can agree that they should be used at all.

Appropriate technology can be defined in a general way as the technology yielding the greatest rate of return. This rate of return can be narrowly defined to include only private benefits, or it can be more broadly defined in terms of social benefits.

It is often assumed that for LDCs, fairly simple labour-intensive technologies are likely to be appropriate. Since LDCs are relatively well-endowed with unskilled labour and relatively short of capital, the opportunity cost of labour is likely to be relatively low, and that of capital, relatively high. Faced with low wage rates and high interest rates, people responsible for choosing between competing technologies are therefore likely maximise both private and social rates of return by choosing technologies at the labour-intensive end of the spectrum.

Box 6.2

Case Study: The Durable Car Company

The Morris Minor motor car was in production in Oxford, England throughout the 1950s and 1960s. There are still 250 000 of these cars in use around the world including 80 000 in the UK. In the city of Bath the Morris Minor Centre is a Mecca for *aficionados* of the Morris Minor. Here, they can find spare parts, get their cars repaired, or purchase a replacement car. The centre is owned by Mr Charles Ware. Over the years Mr Ware purchased sets of Morris Minor design blueprints and machine tools from the Rover Group, and in 1991 he formed a partnership with Mr Dhanapala Samarasekara to build a Morris Minor factory in Sri Lanka. This cost £100 000 to set up, which is a tiny amount in car manufacturing terms. The Durable Car Company was deliberately geared towards labour-intensive production techniques.

Mr Samarasekara stated that the Morris Minor was an ideal car for Sri Lanka because of its reliability, and its 'low-level technology'. There were no expensive and difficult-to-service gadgets such as electronic ignition. If the car needed repair in any part of Sri Lanka, then traditional skills could be used: a broken fan belt, for instance, could be temporarily replaced with a piece of rope. The project had the backing of the Sri Lankan government, who supported its use of local resources. Mr Ware stated that in the factory 95 per cent of operations would be carried out manually, and the plant would use only a minimal amount of electricity. 'We are investing in people,' he said, 'not in machinery.'

Here is an example of the importance to LDCs of both entrepreneurship and appropriate technology.

It is sometimes suggested that small-scale operation is more compatible with existing social and economic structures in LDCs, and is more suitable for rural areas than large-scale production. Thus the debate about appropriate technology often becomes intertwined with a debate about the scale of production.

The great Indian leader, Mahatma Gandhi, was often seen in public carrying a traditional hand-operated spinning-wheel. The Congress Party believed that small-scale businesses and traditional, labour-intensive production methods were preferable to capital-intensive mass-production techniques. However, studies in India and other countries in the 1950s suggested that preserving employment in industries such as textiles and sugar-refining caused costs to rise so that exports declined and jobs were lost.

Traditional economic theory suggests that as a firm grows larger, average costs of production can be lowered by economies of scale. These economies include the ability to use capital-intensive technology, such as mainframe computers or mechanised production lines. In the 1970s, E. F. Schumacher's book *Small is Beautiful* challenged the prevailing economic wisdom that large size could be equated with efficiency.

In becoming more capital-intensive there is a trade-off: an increase in income for a loss of employment. However, it is not necessarily the case that an increase in capital-intensiveness implies an increase in scale, or vice versa.

The scale of operation at a Chinese telephone exchange might be very large indeed; there might be hundreds of operators turning dials and pulling plugs. If labour is relatively cheap, and technology relatively expensive, then it makes sense to use large-scale labour-intensive methods; whereas a British telephone exchange, where machines are relatively cheap and labour is more expensive, can be more appropriately run on capital-intensive lines. Similarly, as technological know-how progresses, many items of technology become more divisible, and available to small firms and large firms alike: whereas twenty years ago only huge corporations could use computers, the development of the microchip and PCs has made computer technology more accessible to small firms. Another important point is that modern technology is often neither capital- nor labour-intensive: it is instead knowledge-intensive. The ability to use computer programs, for instance is, unlike traditional craft skills, relatively easily and quickly communicable by demonstration and the printed word. Provided education and training systems are in place, then a farmer's cooperative in rural Chile could find that the use of a PC to monitor stock control or irrigation flows might well be an appropriate use of technology.

Different choices of technology might imply different patterns of demand for local supplies of factors of production. Technology transferred from MDCs to LDCs might use land or local raw materials, for instance, while making little impact on the demand for labour.

Different choices of technology will also affect the pattern of imports and exports differently. The use of capital-intensive technology is likely to result in an increase in the debit side of balance of payments of LDCs as capital is imported. Increased purchases of capital equipment and other inputs from abroad might increase the dependence of LDCs on their MDC suppliers.

Simpler technologies often produce simpler products suitable for low-income users; complex, capital-intensive technologies may produce complicated products, which are often beyond the reach of local consumers. Inappropriate technology therefore results in inappropriate products.

Different choices of technology will imply different degrees of environmental damage. If there is any doubt as to the importance of appropriate technology to LDCs and MDCs alike, then consider just two words: Chernobyl and Bhopal. The location of a nuclear power station of any description, let alone one of sub-standard design, in a country blessed with huge potential for hydro-electric or coal-fired generation is hardly an example of appropriate technology; neither was the location of a capital-intensive chemical plant in an LDC where the local population was in a position to suffer all the social costs with little or no benefit. The idea of 'making the polluter pay' is not as easy as economics textbooks tend to suggest. In the case of Bhopal it took many years for the Indian authorities to collect evidence and institute proceedings against the company involved. In April 1993 an Indian court ordered eight local officials of the US based Union Carbide company to stand trial for culpable homicide, nine years after deadly gas leaked from the pesticide factory in what has been described as the world's worst industrial accident. The charges involved the deaths of 3828 people.

A basic point is that in assessing the trade-off between income and employment, it is the *nature* of the industry rather than the *size* of the industry which determines whether a certain piece of technology is 'appropriate'.

Multinational Enterprises

A multinational enterprise (MNE) is a business organisation operating in a number of countries. Variously referred to as transnational and multinational corporations or just 'multinationals', these huge organisations have jumped from their domestic bases into more than one economy, to take advantage of differences in factor endowment and government regulation. This gives them the ability to shift activities between locations on a global scale, 'cherry-picking' the location of their operations in such a way as to disadvantage the smaller, local companies which lack the resources to escape their home economies.

MNEs are the main source of foreign direct investment (FDI), which is considered in detail in Chapter 8. Private investment capital moves between countries in two main ways:

1. *Portfolio investment* where the individuals or firms of one country buy stocks and bonds in the organisations of another country mainly for financial gain. They have no more influence than any other shareholder. Britain was the world's dominant portfolio investor in the years before 1914 as private individuals bought railway and municipal stocks all over the world.
2. *FDI* where the firms or residents of one country purchase *and control* an organisation in another country. Any firm that does this becomes an MNE. In the 1950s American companies poured FDI into the world economy, Britain followed after the relaxation of exchange controls in 1979, and in the 1980s Japan became a major source and the USA a recipient of FDI. About three-quarters of FDI is between MDCs, only about a quarter finds its way to LDCs.

The main distinction between the use of the words 'transnational' and 'multinational' in describing these enterprises is one of scale. There are tens of thousands of transnationals with operations in a handful of countries, but multinational enterprises operating in a large number of countries run into the hundreds, and are a far greater influence on global trade and development. By 1985 there were 600 MNEs in mining and manufacturing with a turnover of over one billion dollars. The biggest 74 of them produced over half of the total sales of the 600. These giant firms, such as General Motors, IBM and Unilever enjoy annual turnovers in excess of the GNP of many countries. For example, in 1989 General Motors' three-quarters of a million employees made sales of nearly $127 billion. This exceeded the GDP of 93 of the 112 countries reporting to the *World Development Report* that year, and the country whose GDP came closest (at $126 billion) to GM's sales was Austria.

There has been a rapid growth in the number of MNEs since World War II, and today there are over 35 000 enterprises with production plant, service facilities or foreign affiliates outside their country of origin. Much of the international trade which these companies conduct takes place between the parent firm and its subsidiaries, and according to some estimates this 'intra-firm trade' makes up between 25 and 30 per cent of total world trade. It is often felt that MNEs have been able to race ahead in global operations and decision-making, out of the control of nation-states. It has been alleged that one result of the activities of MNEs is that in many LDCs technology has been transferred from MDCs with insufficient consideration being given as to its appropriateness. The Brandt Commission recommended that there should be increased efforts in both LDCs and MDCs to develop appropriate technology in the light of changed needs regarding both energy and ecology.

MNEs by themselves are unlikely to direct research into areas which do not promise high returns to themselves; there is an urgent need in the MDCs for governments to provide incentives to develop appropriate technologies and make them known to everyone. The question of appropriate technology is relevant to both MDCs and LDCs. Industrialised countries need technologies which conserve energy and non-renewable resources. LDCs need technologies which will improve living standards without driving them into unsustainable debt relationships with MDCs. Both LDCs and MDCs need to face up to the social time bomb of mass unemployment. This requires a greater degree of adaptability among LDCs, and among MDCs a better awareness of the needs of LDCs. It is *possible* that rising energy costs and a greater awareness of the social costs of unemployment will trigger, through market forces, a switch towards appropriate technology as a matter of 'enlightened self-interest'; but *more likely* that national and international conscious action is required if any real progress is to be made in the foreseeable future.

MNEs and LDCs

Why would MNEs become interested in LDCs ? The first argument that springs to the economist's mind involves factor costs: most LDCs have large amounts of labour available at low wages, while the MNE has access to the capital markets of the developed world. British Airways' recent decision to move some of its administration to India is a good example.

As far as markets for final goods are concerned, it surely makes more sense for MNEs to sell in the MDCs where disposable incomes are higher. This is not necessarily the case. The world market for laundry detergents, toothpaste, toilet paper and other household goods is an oligopoly dominated by MNEs such as Unilever, and Procter and Gamble. In the MDCs these household products are income inelastic: a 20 per cent increase in income will not lead to a proportionate increased consumption of toothpaste, for example. But, according to Procter and Gamble's chief executive, annual consumption of toilet paper in the USA averages 53.5 rolls per person per annum compared with 22.5 rolls in Mexico and 4.3 rolls in Eastern Europe. Development allows such products to be income elastic in the long run, as LDCs catch up with MDC levels of consumption, helped by advertising campaigns and branding that play on 'standards for emulation'. This enabled the chief executive to promise investors that Procter and Gamble would double its 1996 sales in ten years, and would do so again in the next ten years by expanding its markets in LDCs.

Coca-Cola and McDonald's provide equally powerful evidence: America's 266 million people consumed an average of 363 Coca-Cola drinks each in 1996, while the Chinese drank an average of five. Remembering that China's population is 1.23 billion, the average needs to rise only a little to guarantee growth to the company. This explains why $40 invested in the company in 1919 was worth over $6.6m by mid-1997. McDonald's recently overtook Coca-Cola as the world's best known brand despite the fact that it serves less than 1 per cent of the world's population on any given day. Such MNEs have plenty of growth potential in the LDC markets. Now that action is being taken against tobacco companies in MDCs, their growth can continue through expansion in LDC markets too. MNEs are perpetual growth machines in LDCs even if demand for their products is income inelastic in MDCs.

Why should LDCs be interested in attracting MNEs ? It can be argued, in favour of MNE activity in the LDCs, that they help to close the development gap by overcoming the shortfall between domestic saving and the desired level of investment. Allowing FDI enables the host LDC to reach economies of scale, and perhaps minimum efficient scale for overseas trade more quickly: helping an LDC with balance-of-payments problems. This is particularly the case if the MNE generates exports whose earnings contribute significantly to GDP. However, export earnings might be offset by imports of raw materials and component parts from within the MNE's other operations; this is especially true of 'screwdriver' operations, where in order to benefit from cheap labour and have access to regional markets, the MNE uses its plant merely to complete the assembly of a final product, keeping the higher-grade technology at home. Massey Ferguson, for example, sends tractors in 'knock-down kit' form from its British headquarters in Coventry for completion in the Middle East. Most of the value added remains in Britain. It must also be remembered that an MNE will generate a 'once and for all' inflow of capital at the time FDI occurs and subsequent outflows in the form of repatriated profits.

MNEs can have a multiplier effect on the local economy, creating jobs not only in the MNE itself, but in industries with which it deals, and in the local economy where its employees spend their new disposable incomes. MNEs are also are a useful source of tax revenue for the government of the host country, and if part of this revenue is spent on such things as infrastructure projects (spending which lowers the costs of economic activity to all, such as improving transport and communications) the multiplier effect can be greater still. MNEs can also give a boost to education and training in the host country, since they will have training schemes and might encourage local people to acquire entrepreneurial and managerial skills. Overall, in the best of all possible worlds, MNEs tend to benefit LDCs by focusing on areas of comparative or absolute advantage, and stimulating efficiency and competition.

On the other hand, the impact of the MNE might be skewed towards one sector of the community at the expense of others; 60 per cent of MNEs are to be found in manufacturing, and three-quarters of the hundred largest have their headquarters in just five MDCs – France, Germany, Japan, the USA and the UK. Thus to attract the MNE, it is necessary for the LDC to be following an industrialisation pathway to development and to enjoy the confidence of investors in these five countries. Once established, the MNE might increase incomes for only a small group of people, thus widening income inequality. Tax revenues might not be as great as expected; MNEs can use their size to negotiate tax concessions, and being relatively mobile they might threaten to move elsewhere if such concessions are not given. Being large and monopolistic, they might actually stifle entrepreneurship in the host country by discouraging competition and importing their own managers. They might use inappropriate technology, such as capital-intensive methods in an area of high unemployment and low wages. Their training might be in inappropriate skills, or in skills which are at a relatively low level. The tourist industry, for example, is often said to be destined to become the world's largest employer. It is not unknown for a hotel chain investing in an LDC to import its own management and employ local people in positions such as porters and cleaners. In such a case the host country can do a lot to counteract this tendency by developing vocational training within its educational system so that more of its population can compete for higher grade jobs. Finally, MNEs often promote unsuitable products, or create unreal preferences through their persuasive advertising. In MDCs branding is an accepted feature of oligopolistic non-price competition, but selling expensive branded carbonated drinks to countries where access to fresh water is not widely established is inappropriate.

MNEs in the 1990s

In the 1960s, the power of MNEs to shift profits to tax havens and research and development (R&D) to wherever it was subsidised, was seen as a threat to individual countries' power over their own economic management. The American headquarters of most MNEs together with the dollar's dominance and the IMF's supervision of the exchange rate system were taken as suspicious signs of a new US economic and cultural imperialism. There was therefore hostility to FDI in the 1970s in some countries, such as Japan. In the 1980s the climate improved and as FDI grew between the MDCs in the 1990s, the LDCs began to fear being left out. In 1995 the four biggest recipients of FDI were the USA, Britain, France and Australia, with the USA absorbing $60 billion and Britain $30 billion out of a global total of

$318 billion. Only parts of Latin America, the Asian Tigers, China and some former communist countries in Central and Eastern Europe could compete to attract FDI. Africa lags far behind.

At the same time MNEs became less centralised and autocratic, fostering looser forms of relationship with local LDC firms such as joint ventures and licensing agreements. To overcome earlier suspicion they have also set themselves ethical standards drawn from the value systems of their MDC customers. There are dangers in this: consumer boycotts over the sinking of the Brent Spar oil rig and involvement in Nigeria have hurt Shell, while pressure groups have attacked any MNEs operating in Myanmar on human rights grounds or mining in Irian Jaya, Indonesia, on environmental grounds. This shows that maintaining ethical standards is not easy in a world where public scrutiny of MNE activities is better organised. Pressure groups like Greenpeace, which has offices in 33 countries, now take MNEs to court in MDCs for their actions in LDCs, and are adept at lobbying shareholders. A recent survey in *The Economist* gave examples of MNEs' responses to criticisms of their activities in environmentally sensitive areas: these include Chevron paying the Worldwide Fund for Nature to preserve forest in Papua New Guinea, and Shell discussing in advance the development of a gas field in Peru with indigenous people and 60 governmental and pressure groups.

The economic principle that underlays the growth of MNEs, *economies of scale*, may have started to work against them in the 1990s. As customers demand goods to match their particular market and tastes, standardised products have become less popular. Where car companies used to produce the same model in similar factories in different countries whose markets were separated by protectionism, the arrival of computer-controlled production, *just in time* production and freer trade has led to production lines which rarely produce two identical models in a production run of a hundred. Economies of scale are less important than mass producing goods customised to the needs of each individual consumer. MNEs' most valuable resource may not be their size but the knowledge of how to manage the mass production of personalised consumer goods.

Trade and Development

7

What does international trade offer the LDC – a threat or an opportunity? As usual in economics, the answer is a mixture of both depending on a series of secondary factors. The relationship between an LDC and the trading world is dependent on its factor endowment, its political attitudes to trading partners and MNEs, and its recent economic history. For example, the discovery of oil, the joining of a trade bloc, or the ending of an imperial relationship could all make differences to the level of welfare in the country.

International trade *can* increase welfare. It therefore follows that an understanding of international trading relationships is absolutely crucial to future progress of the LDCs. Why does trade take place?

David Ricardo (1772–1823) showed how international trade depends on the law of comparative costs, which states that countries will specialise in the production of goods and services in which they have a comparative advantage. It is important to distinguish between *absolute* and *comparative advantage*. A country has an absolute advantage over another in the production of a good or service if, with a given amount of resources, it can produce more than the other country, or if it can produce the same amount with fewer resources. Comparative advantage is more subtle, and sometimes far less obvious. Whereas absolute advantage exists where an item is produced at a lower absolute cost, a country has a comparativ e advantage if it can produce a good at a lower domestic opportunity cost than another good, compared with the same two goods in another country. The

Ricardian model suggests that total world output, incomes, and hence living standards, can increase if countries specialise in producing goods and services in which they enjoy comparative advantage. In essence, it takes Adam Smith's principle of division of labour, and shows how specialisation and trade can benefit countries as well as individuals. Numerical illustrations of this proposition can be found in many textbooks.

The point of trade is to allow countries to specialise in those goods and services in which absolute or comparative advantage exists. Economists are generally convinced of the virtues of free trade, but the laws of absolute and comparative advantage work best in a world which is 'frictionless': without transport and exchange rate costs, and in which countries are willing to trade on equal, open terms.

Countries which are intentionally open to world markets, such as the Asian Tigers, are described as *outward orientated*, while those which protect their domestic markets from the blast of foreign competition and try to develop using their own resources are described as *inward orientated*. Increasingly, in the 1990s, the appearance of *trade blocs* allows an LDC aspects of outward orientation in its relationship with fellow members inside a *free trade area, customs union* or *common market*, while keeping some insulation against the extreme competition of world markets.

The Sectoral Balance and Economies of Scale

Most LDCs regard industrialisation as a major objective of economic policy, and as something which will close the gap in living standards between them and the MDCs. If an industrial sector is to be developed, the immediate problem is that most LDCs lack the market size to foster an industry that could be competitive in world markets. This is because most industrialised production involves economies of scale that must be achieved before exporting is possible. In Figure 7.1, the *long run average cost curve* (LRAC) is shown falling as a result of economies of scale to the same level as world market prices at output O_{it}. In this case, it takes the whole of the domestic market and this implies substantial output. Expanding output further, the LRAC falls below $P_w S_w$ and the LDC can export competitively. Remembering that MNEs may already have access to many markets at the same time, it is particularly hard for the industrial sector of one country to reach the 'efficient' international trading threshold, shown as O_{it} in Figure 7.1. Procter and Gamble estimates the number of consumers within its reach has grown from 1 billion in 1987 to 4.5 billion in 1997, and that is four times the population of China. It can enjoy economies of scale far beyond the limits of its domestic market in the USA.

FIGURE 7.1
LDC Industrial Output and World Markets

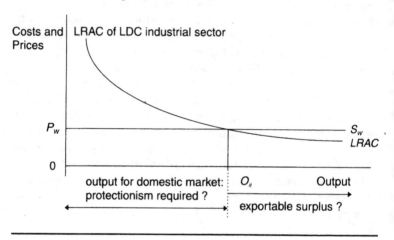

KEY

LRAC = Long Run Average Cost Curve
$P_w S_w$ = World Supply Curve at World Supply Price
O_{it} = Minimum output level that must be reached to allow LDC
         output costs to be internationally competitive

The only countries whose industries have reached this efficient threshold across a broad range of industrial products in the last thirty years are known as the *newly industrialised countries* (NICs), including the 'Asian Tigers' (Taiwan, Malaysia, Hong Kong, South Korea and Singapore), together with Brazil, Mexico, Saudi Arabia and India. All have had substantial home markets or high income per head compared with their rivals. Already, the 12 leading NICs account for over 15 per cent of world trade in manufactures.

Some LDCs have given priority to the improvement of their agricultural sector, while others have used industrialisation as the central instrument of development. There need not be a conflict between the priorities of agriculture and industry in a nation's development. They remain closely interdependent, with the income and production from one providing the demand for the other. One of the most crucial tasks for the governments of LDCs is to manage the balance between agriculture and industry and to provide healthy conditions for both sectors. In ideal circumstances, the agricultural sector will improve its productivity, releasing labour from the land to seek employment in the new industrial sector. The extent to which they succeed is closely related to the international economic environment. Thus a downturn in the economies of the MDCs indirectly causes an increase in the size of shanty towns in LDCs.

Outward Orientation

One approach to development is to concentrate on producing exports from the industrial sector. Adam Smith recognised as long ago as 1776 that specialisation, trade, exchange and hence the 'Wealth of Nations' was limited by what he called the *extent of the market*. Singapore (population: 3.0 million) and Hong Kong (6.2 million), both rich city-states, have relatively small but affluent domestic markets, and so if they were to produce manufactured goods solely for the domestic market they would not benefit from mass production techniques. Instead, they manufacture far more than they can consume themselves, and export the surplus. Even countries like Korea (44.9 million in 1995) and Malaysia (21 million) have had to concentrate on export demand, because the home market is too small to produce sufficient economies of scale. This is done despite knowing that such a policy might worsen inequalities of income, since cheap labour is an important element in the international competitiveness of these countries. Outward orientation means being open to foreign employers who are looking specifically for compliant and cheap labour markets with minimal regulations.

The NICs have for many years exported items such as textiles and clothing to the MDCs, but they have more recently begun to develop markets for products such as steel, consumer goods, petrochemicals, electronics and cars. Often the know-how, design and technology is imported from MDCs such as Japan, and combined with cheap labour which undercuts the wage costs of the MDCs by a margin with which producers in the MDCs can never hope to compete. The success of the

Proton car in the UK is a case in point; designed in Japan and based on Japanese technology, but built in Malaysia it provides a five-door family saloon at under £8000; at this price there is virtually no competition, except from other products of the Asian Tigers. Kia, Daewoo, Mahindra, Ssanyong and the Proton actually penetrated the British car market during the worst part of the UK recession in the early 1990s.

A potential problem is that outward orientation puts LDCs at the mercy of changing world conditions. A world recession can cause export volumes to shrink, make the prices of exports unreliable, lead to protectionism on export markets, and cause difficulty in repaying the loans that made industrialisation possible through purchasing fuel and machinery. In the MDCs, the real or imagined threat from the NICs might also provoke allegations of *dumping*, or flooding their markets with goods at an 'unfairly' low price, and might prompt some sort of retaliation in the form of protectionism.

Inward Orientation

Countries like China and India until the early 1990s, with a large domestic market, and with many natural resources of their own, have been able to pursue a policy of exporting a great deal less than many other NICs, while meeting their own needs and replacing many imports with local products. In India, the domestic car market, for example, was not served by the multinationals like Ford and General Motors whose products are so well known in the MDCs. Instead of the Ford Escort, Indian streets are still thronged with the Hindustan Ambassador, a locally built version of the Morris Oxford, a well known British car of the 1950s.

Smaller countries experience serious difficulties with this approach. This is again because of the limited extent of the market (there might be too few customers to make up a mass market, or there might be many potential customers without the economic means to buy the products); or because of a lack of local resources, making the country dependent on imported raw materials which need to be paid for through exports.

Import substitution can also lead to stresses and strains when consumers demand access to goods and services which have become internationalised; in an age of worldwide telecommunications consumers everywhere are aware of the existence of Levi jeans, McDonald hamburgers, Cadbury's chocolate and Timotei shampoo, and might not be willing to accept a locally produced alternative. Some commentators have gone so far as to suggest that the idea of the Volkswagen Golf replacing the Trabant played as much a part in the destruction of the Berlin Wall as the desire for wider freedoms. This might seem extreme, but the advertising and branding activities of oligopolistic firms engaged in non-price competition are perceived throughout the world, and often give rise to *standards for emulation*. This is a belief on the part of consumers in LDCs that possession of branded goods from MDCs confers status. This explains why formula milk for babies and western cigarette brands can increase sales in LDCs although they actually arouse disapproval in their countries of origin. The association between Michael Jackson and Pepsi in the eighties sent a global signal about branding to the youth of LDCs. The Spice Girls and The Prodigy may be transient phenomena, but both incorporate their sponsors' names (Pepsi and Ballantine's Whisky) in the marketing of their world tours. Keeping such brands out of a market through protectionism when they are associated with cultural icons can cause a government serious unpopularity.

An advantage of the inward strategy is that it avoids problems associated with international payments and indebtedness; however, there are powerful arguments based in economic theory for an open economy geared up towards trade.

Trade and Welfare

In what ways can economic welfare be increased by international trade? Figure 7.2 shows the market for a good in a closed economy; that is, an economy that does not take part in international trade. The good in question could be, for example, socks; and the diagram shows the familiar supply and demand equilibrium. One way of attempting to measure economic welfare through trade is to consider the 'balance' between *consumer surplus* and *producer surplus*. The demand curve can be regarded as indicating the maximum amount which consumers are willing to pay for the right to purchase a product. The difference between what the consumer is willing to pay and the actual price paid can be thought of as being 'free' satisfaction, or consumer surplus. If the equilibrium price is P_E, then every consumer to the left of Q_E receives consumer surplus and the total consumer surplus received is equal to area $P_E BE$. In economic theory, the rational consumer is said to desire maximum utility, and so an increase in consumer surplus can be taken to mean an increase in welfare.

FIGURE 7.2
International Trade and Economic Welfare: A Closed Economy without International Trade

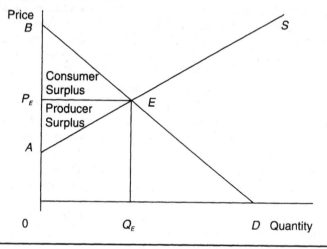

KEY

P_E	=	Price
Q_E	=	Quantity bought and sold
$P_E BE$	=	Consumer surplus
$AP_E E$	=	Product surplus
$0P_E EQ_E$	=	Producer revenue / total expenditure

The supply curve can be taken to indicate the minimum return which is necessary to induce a producer to supply a product. Any surplus over and above this minimum return can be referred to as producer surplus. Producer surplus in Figure 7.2 is shown by area $AP_E E$. The theory of perfect competition makes much of the idea that although producers act in their own self-interest in trying to maximise short-run profits, in the long run competition ensures that surplus profits disappear, and this is said to encourage an optimum use of resources. We can therefore conclude that a reduction in producer surplus is likely correspond to an improved allocation of resources, and hence an increase in welfare.

FIGURE 7.3
International Trade and Economic Welfare: An Open Economy with International Trade

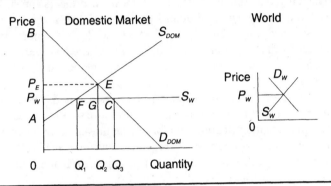

KEY

S_{DOM} = Domestic Supply Curve
D_{DOM} = Domestic Demand Curve
P_E = Equilibrium Price in the Domestic Market without World Trade
$P_W S_W$ = World Supply Curve at World price
D_W = World Demand Curve
S_W = World Supply Curve in the World Market

Figure 7.3 shows the market for socks after the closed economy has become an 'open' one, that is, after international trade starts to take place. The price is determined on the world market, where the world price, P_W is established at the intersection of the world supply curve, S_W, and world demand, D_W. The world price is lower than the domestically determined price, reflecting the greater efficiency of foreign producers over some but not all domestic producers, and the greater market size.

From the domestic point of view, the world price line appears as a horizontal supply curve, $P_W S_W$. Assuming that this line is horizontal tells us two things. Firstly, it suggests that domestic production, S_{DOM}, is small compared with world supply, so that domestic producers cannot by their own actions affect world price. They therefore act as 'price takers'. Secondly, it suggests that domestic consumers could have their entire demand satisfied by suppliers in the rest of the world: to domestic consumers an infinite quantity can be bought at the world price.

The world price P_W now acts as a ceiling price on domestic producers, because if they tried to charge their equilibrium price P_E, they would sell nothing, and consumers would only purchase cheaper imports. Hence only the most efficient domestic producers can survive. They sell quantity $0Q_1$, and quantity Q_1Q_3 represents imports. Producer surplus falls from AP_EE to AP_WF, while consumer surplus increases from P_EBE to P_WBC. Consumer welfare has therefore increased, as a result of the transfer of some producer surplus to consumer surplus.

However, a different sort of welfare has also accrued. The opening of the market has enabled consumers to buy more socks than before at a lower price: market clearing equilibrium has moved down the demand curve from E to C. Home consumers gained consumer surplus P_WP_EEF from home producers, but where did the triangles FEG and GEC come from? FEG is consumer surplus arising from the transfer of production from less efficient home to more efficient world market producers (a 'green' gain from the more efficient use of the world's resources); GEC is a *gain to society* that has not involved a transfer from anyone – socks are cheaper and therefore more widely consumed. It could also be argued that welfare has increased in other ways, since consumers are likely to find that through having imported socks made available to them they have greater choice of materials, styles, and so on.

Protectionism and Welfare

In the real world of international trade the choice is not just whether to be outward or inward orientated.

Countries may have as many trade policies as they have exports and imports, and no nation follows a policy of free trade in all goods and services. Since 1945 the average level of tariffs (import duties) has fallen substantially in trade between MDCs, from 40 per cent to less than five per cent, but protectionism has taken on many new forms despite the clear arguments for economic liberalism advocated by most economists since Adam Smith.

FIGURE 7.4
The Welfare Implications of a Tariff in Closed, Protected and Free Trading Economies

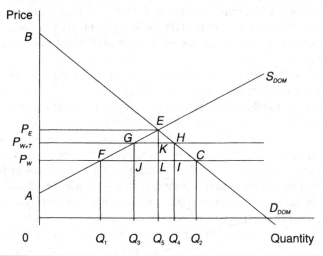

KEY

(Assuming movement from closed to protected to free trade economy)

Economy	Closed Economy →	Protected Economy →	Free Trade
Equilibrium Price and Quantity	P_E, Q_5	P_{W+T}, Q_4	P_W
Domestic Consumer Surplus	$P_E BE$	$P_{W+T} BH$	$P_W BC$
Domestic Producer Surplus	$AP_E E$	$AP_{W+T} G$	$AP_W F$
'Green' Gain	–	GEK	FEL
Gain for Society	–	KEH	LEC
Government Revenue	–	$JGHI$	–

Protectionism consists mainly of tariffs, quotas, voluntary export restraints, embargoes, subsidies, import licenses, local content agreements, health and safety legislation (sometimes spurious) and international commodity agreements. Countries may selectively drop some of these measures to chosen partners (the first steps towards a trade bloc), or they may even combine the above measures. Australia, for example has used 'tariff-quotas' in footwear, clothing and textiles: a predetermined quantity is imported at a standard tariff, and beyond this quota importers pay higher penalty-rate tariffs. For LDCs trying to break into the markets of MDCs this can be bewildering.

Figure 7.4 shows the welfare implications of one of the main methods of protectionism or restricting trade, the imposition of a tariff, or a specific tax on imported goods. Three positions are shown in the diagram: a closed economy with no trade; a protected economy which trades with a tariff; and a free trade economy. Moving from the closed economy to trading with a tariff, and from there to free trade increases welfare in two stages. Moving from free trade towards protectionism and the closed economy reduces welfare. There are transfers between producer surplus and consumer surplus, as well as 'green' gains and losses, and gains and deadweight losses for society. These are summarised in the key below Figure 7.4. Also, the tariff is not just a means of protecting home industry – it raises revenue for government, and this can be used to keep domestic direct and indirect taxes down. For LDCs in the early stages of development, without a substantial taxable working population, protective tariffs are a relatively painless form of indirect taxation, yet the welfare gains denied are clear.

Figure 7.5 shows an import quota scheme which allows only a limited quantity of goods to be imported. Let us assume the country starts with free trade: domestic output is $0Q_1$ and imports at the world price (P_W) are Q_1Q_2. The supply curve is AB, then horizontal until it crosses the demand curve at d_1. If the government imposes a quota equal to BC, in effect the supply curve becomes horizontal between the quota limits before continuing its upward path as a domestic supply curve only, but parallel to its original course. Thus its course is $ABCD$, with AB and Cd_2 supplied by domestic producers and BC by foreign producers. At d_2, where the demand curve is crossed, a new price level P_Q is established. Thus the quota has similar welfare effects to a tariff, except that the extra revenue that results from the higher price goes to the importer or foreign producer instead of the home government as tax revenue. From the foreign producer's point of view, the introduction of the quota has cost the lost opportunity to export Q_3Q_2, but he has gained extra revenue FEd_2G. Exporters have less to lose from quotas than they do from tariffs. *BEF* is a 'green' loss, representing the waste of resources that occurs because Q_1Q_4 is now produced by less efficient home producers, and Gd_2d_1 is a deadweight loss to society resulting from higher prices and a market that has shrunk from Q_2 to Q_5.

FIGURE 7.5
The Welfare Effects of a Quota

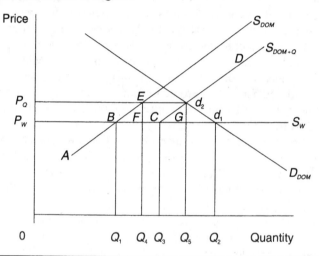

KEY

ABd_1 = Supply Curve under Free Trade
$ABCd_2$ = Supply Curve with Quota
FEd_2G = Extra Revenue to Foreign Producers
BEF = 'Green Loss'
Gd_2d_1 = Deadweight Welfare Loss

New Protectionism

For LDCs the implications of the forms of protectionism considered so far are twofold. *Firstly*, use of protectionism by LDCs is discouraged by the IMF whose economic liberalism is powerfully expressed in the *structural adjustment programmes* imposed on LDCs in balance of payments difficulties. Conditionality in IMF loans usually involved forcible outward orientation. Yet the powerful MDCs so dominate international organisations like the IMF and the World Trade Organisation (WTO) that their protectionism is tolerated. For example, the *Multi-Fibre Agreement* (MFA) of 1961 was a short-term arrangement of bilateral quotas on LDC exports of cotton textiles to the MDCs. It became a long-term spider's web of protectionism covering many clothing and textile products, and will remain operative until early in the next century. A tariff is a general barrier for any country's products to climb – the MFA actually specifies the countries whose exports are subject to quotas, so the welfare effects are targeted rather than generalised. *Secondly*, use of protectionism by MDCs against LDC products is more subtle than the tariff or quota. These can now be considered part of 'old protectionism' of a type that is in long-term decline: the GATT rounds of multilateral trade negotiations helped the USA to reduce average tariffs from 50 to five per cent, and Britain from 40 to four per cent since 1945. But the 1980s and 1990s have seen the rise of non-tariff barriers often specific to particular products or sources. The World Bank estimates that about 15 per cent of EU imports are subject to some form of non-tariff barrier. 'New protectionism' is much harder for the LDCs to overcome.

Not only do exporters have less to lose from quotas than tariffs, there is the possibility of higher prices for the quota more than compensating for the lost market share. This would be likely if the demand curve were particularly steep, reflecting inelasticity of demand for the import. Figure 7.6 shows the *voluntary export restraints* (VERs) such as those negotiated between the UK and Japanese car exporters. Here the foreign producer, in an act of apparent consideration towards the less efficient home producers, imposes a quota Q_1 upon himself, forcing the supply curve to turn vertical and cross the domestic demand curve at a much higher price P_{VER}, thus boosting his own revenues. The revenue box $0P_{VER}AQ_1$ is clearly larger than $0P_WBQ_2$, and the higher prices paid by consumers result in a deadweight loss to society of CAB and a transfer of revenues to foreign producers of $P_WP_{VER}AC$. One result of VERs in Europe in recent years is that Japanese car producers have chosen to satisfy fully demand for luxury and sports cars which have larger profit margins but smaller sales, while not importing the small and inexpensive city cars that are typical of Japanese cities.

By self-limiting imports, the Japanese can claim to have preserved jobs in Britain, but the opportunity cost is the vastly higher price paid for Japanese cars by those who buy them.

FIGURE 7.6
The Voluntary Export Restraint

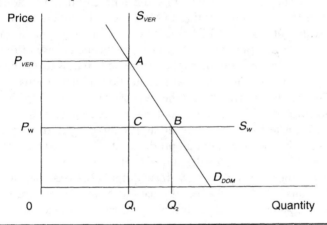

KEY

BC	=	VER
P_wS_w	=	World Price and World Supply Curve
P_{VER}	=	Price after VER is introduced
$0P_wBQ_2$	=	Revenue to the Producer before the VER is introduced
$0P_{VER}AQ_1$	=	Revenue to the Producer after the VER is Introduced
CAB	=	Deadweight Loss to Society

Medium-sized cars for the mass market are increasingly assembled in 'transplants', such as the Nissan, Toyota and Honda plants in Sunderland, Derby and Swindon. The aim is to avoid protectionism by moving production inside the Common External Tariff of the EU. Cars are only assembled in these places – the thousands of components are manufactured elsewhere and this might offer an opportunity for LDCs to make small engineered parts or sub-assemblies. However, *local content agreements* specify a fixed percentage of the car's components must be locally produced. This has proved important in preserving the automotive engineering sector in Australia, for example, which otherwise might have lost employment to the Asian Tigers.

Buying Competitiveness: Subsidies

Governments engage in a form of protectionism when they take steps to give inefficient domestic producers the illusion of competitiveness at world market prices by subsidising production or by subsiding exports. This is, in effect a fiscal, non-tariff barrier. MDCs can use the power of their taxpayers to do this where LDCs can not. Trade blocs such as the EU, incorporating 15 MDCs, can do this on an even bigger scale. Although GATT limited the use of direct payments of subsidies from governments to their own producers, the use of regional policy to stimulate employment in depressed areas is really the same thing as a production subsidy with protectionist implications.

This can be illustrated with the help of Figure 7.7. The aim of the production subsidy is to raise domestic production from $0Q_1$ to $0Q_2$. Its effect is to move the domestic supply curve S_{DOM} to the right (as the subsidy is so much per unit produced) to S_{SUB}. Producers receive the world price P_W, plus the subsidy which is the vertical distance between the two supply curves: AD at output Q_2. Consumers are able to buy quantity Q_3 at the world price P_W, of which home producers supply $0Q_2$ and foreign producers Q_2Q_3. Home producers receive a subsidy $P_W P_{SUB} AD$.

How does this differ from the use of a tariff? Of course, the government pays a subsidy rather than receiving tariff revenue, but there is also a welfare effect. The subsidy does not cause the price to rise from P_W, so the size of the market remains at $0Q_3$, and there is no deadweight loss to society. Nevertheless domestic production and employment equal to Q_1Q_2 has been 'bought' from more efficient foreign producers using the power of the taxpayers who fund government spending. LDCs lack such a taxpaying base and therefore are pushed back to reliance on tariffs, the 'old protectionism' so discouraged by international organisations like GATT and the IMF. Until the early 1990s the EU used regionally variable production subsidies in the lamb market, the ostensible aim being to preserve hill farming, but the effect being to discourage imports from the southern hemisphere.

An *intervention purchasing scheme*, such as that of the Common Agricultural Policy of the European Union, sets prices at a 'floor' level, intended to guarantee farmers' incomes, then forces prices up to this level by the government purchasing the surplus output created. This can act as a restriction of free trade, since cheaper imports will not be allowed to undermine the floor price. A 'setaside' or production quota scheme limits the amount which domestic producers can produce by maintaining a floor price by shifting the domestic supply curve to the left. Both these measures will require a protective tariff to prevent the floor price being undermined by more efficient producers abroad.

FIGURE 7.7
The Welfare Effects of a Production Subsidy

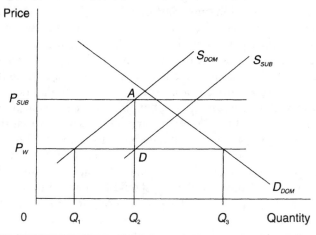

KEY

Before subsidy:
$0Q_1$ = Domestically supplied
Q_1Q_3 = Imports
After subsidy:
AD = Subsidy at output Q_2
$0Q_2$ = Domestically supplied
Q_2Q_3 = Imports
$P_WP_{SUB}AD$ = Cost to government

In all of these cases some welfare is transferred between different groups (consumers, domestic producers, foreign producers, the government), and it can be argued that this does at least mean that the total amount of welfare is maintained, although it is redistributed. However, in each case except the subsidy there is also a deadweight loss to society, i.e. a loss of welfare which is not transferred but disappears into thin air reducing the total sum of human welfare. This explains why economists generally prefer subsidies to tariffs, quotas and VERs if protectionism is inevitable.

Free Trade versus Protectionism: Infant Industries and Dumping

Why, then, is it sometimes argued that free trade *should* be suspended, and that protectionism can be justified?

Governments argue that it is necessary to protect certain *strategic industries* from competition. This is a political argument, rather than being solely economic, because the decision to define a certain industry as 'strategic' cannot be made on purely economic grounds. In a continent with a warlike history, it is not surprising that defence industries such as aircraft and shipbuilding have been heavily subsidised and protected from foreign competition. The fact that the EU countries protect their agricultural sector, for example, has more to do with the history and politics of Europe than it has to do with economic principles. In terms of economic efficiency, it is absurd that 60 per cent of the budget of the EU should be devoted to an industry which employs 4 per cent of the population, that the EU commission should spend taxpayers' money on maintaining surpluses of expensive farm products, and that farmers and fishermen should attack imports on the grounds that they are too cheap. If we trace the history of the EU, however, to the immediate post-war years when there were shortages of food in the countries of western Europe, then we can understand how, at that time, food production was seen as a strategic industry, worthy of special treatment, even if that treatment discouraged imports and contravened Ricardian principles. Yet the result is that heavily subsidised, low-quality tobacco enters the world market from Europe at prices that create the illusion of competitiveness, and keeps potentially more efficient but unsubsidised farmers in LDCs out of trade.

It is sometimes said that *infant industries* need protection. This is an economic argument for temporary protectionism: the government of an LDC might be tempted to protect some of its manufacturers, for example, believing that until they reach a certain size they cannot compete with established manufacturers who benefit from economies of scale. On the other hand, it is argued that the capital market should be capable of taking a view which is sufficiently long term to make protection unnecessary. As long as the long-term gains from trade outweigh the short-term costs of protectionism, an infant industry worth supporting will obtain that support, and so there is no need for the government to involve itself in 'picking winners'.

At the other end of the life-cycle of businesses, there are some *declining industries*; in the MDCs these include textiles and deep mining for coal, in the LDCs they include the production of hemp and sisal, whose markets have been invaded by man-made products. The social costs of declining industries, which include unemployment, might tempt governments to try to support such industries through protection from international competition. This denies consumers the opportunity to purchase these products at world prices; many economists argue that the social costs are more efficiently reduced by 'targeting', that is by subsidising the industries affected. An economic determinist would argue that industries in structural decline should be allowed to decline and free their resources for profitable use as quickly as possible.

Dumping is a practice which sometimes leads to calls for protection. Dumping occurs when foreign producers sell goods in domestic markets at below the cost of production. 'Theory of the firm' tells us that this is a short-run phenomenon, and it is indeed usually explained by disposal of surpluses, the end of a production run, or the establishment of a brand identity. It is most likely during recessions. Dumping is harmful, especially when it is done by large multinationals in small markets with local producers, and for this reason GATT was willing to allow temporary departures from its freer trade ambitions to deal with it.

The difficulty with dumping is in establishing what the level of production cost really is. Suppose a manufacturing firm in an LDC finds that if it doubles its output of men's suits it can benefit from economies of scale, and so increase its profit margin on each suit sold. It might find that it does not have the market locally for the extra production, and so will divert the extra suits on to the export market at prices which only just cover costs. These prices could well be extremely low when compared with prices charged by manufacturers in MDCs, due to the cheaper labour costs. This might not technically be dumping in the strict sense of selling below the costs of production, but the prices might be so low as to lead to this impression. Local consumers, of course, will not complain about low-priced imports; in fact, they will welcome them – unless, of course, they find themselves out of a job as a result. The problem here is to distinguish between dumping and the legitimate selling of goods at a lower price which reflects lower costs. Footballs sewn by children in Bangladesh are cheaper than UK footballs because of low labour costs, but the 'cheap labour' argument merges into MDC arguments that some types of competition are unfair, morally questionable and therefore justify protectionism.

In all cases of trade restraints which are not negotiated, and which are therefore not voluntary, any argument in favour must be weighed against the ever-present and potentially devastating possibility of *retaliation*, destroying export markets for all countries.

'Frictionless' Trade for LDCs?

Because of their limited industrial capacity LDCs miss out on the earnings to be made by processing commodities and turning them into manufactured products. 'Value added' tends to accrue towards the end of the production process, closer to the markets in the MDCs. A wider industrial base would enable LDCs to make a greater share of the profits. We can identify certain features of the market for the items which typically occur in the international trading relationships of the LDCs which pose particular problems for these countries.

As described in Chapter 5, the *terms of trade index* is calculated from the ratio of export prices to import prices. If the prices on world markets of a country's exports rise more quickly (or fall more slowly) than its import prices, then this signifies an improvement in the terms of trade. It means that a given quantity of exports can be exchanged for a greater quantity of imports.

It is generally assumed that the terms of trade of LDCs largely depend on the terms of trade for primary products (commodities), and that there is a tendency for the terms of trade to deteriorate. This assumption is largely due to the work of the Argentinean economist Raul Prebisch, who used UN statistics to support his view that the terms of trade of LDCs have deteriorated steadily throughout the twentieth century. Apart from the boom period for commodities during and immediately after World War II, the trend is indeed very marked. Taking 1980 as the base year (100) real commodity prices deflated by the price of manufactures fell from 130 in 1950 to below 70 by 1988.

Other economists have argued that this trend might be true for individual countries, but it is not necessarily always true for all LDCs. At one extreme an African or Asian country whose only significant export is, for example, tea, and which imports virtually everything else, is likely to find its terms of trade deteriorating. This is because the price of tea rises only very slowly on world markets, and might even fall, while the price of everything else rises much more quickly. This country therefore has to export more and more tea to pay for its imports of everything else. Countries specialising in the supply of jute, sisal, or rubber would have had similar experiences at various times in recent history. In 1990 sub-Saharan African countries' merchandise exports consisted of 84 per cent fuels, minerals, metals and other primary products, with only 16 per cent machinery, transport equipment and other manufactures. At the other extreme, an Asian Tiger such as South Korea might have expected to escape the effects of the long-term decline in commodity terms of trade with seven per cent commodity and 93 per cent manufactures in its merchandise exports. Oil exporting LDCs have also escaped the decline in commodity terms of trade, especially in the 1970s and early 1980s.

Commodity Trade

Countries whose export earnings depend heavily on a narrow range of primary products have long considered world market arrangements unsatisfactory. Prices are volatile, exchange rates unpredictable (especially since the early 1970s) and the new protectionism leads to uncertainties. No long-term solutions have been found, but two distinct attempts have been made: the first involves *supply limitation*, and the second *commodity agreements*.

In the 1930s Brazil had a near monopoly of world coffee supplies. When nearly all commodity prices fell in the wake of the great depression of 1929–32, Brazil destroyed coffee stocks by burning them. Reducing supply during a period of weak demand caused prices to rise as demand recovered, attracting many new suppliers and causing the loss of Brazil's dominant position. An international attempt to limit the supply of oil is considered below.

BOX 7.1

Case Study: The Tin Collapse

In October 1985 trading of tin on the London Metal Exchange was suspended when the International Tin Council (ITC), representing twenty-two producing countries, announced that it was withdrawing as a purchaser, while owing about £900m to brokers and banks.

During the 1970s, tin was in short supply because of political disturbances in some of the producing countries, and the exhaustion of reserves in others. This caused prices to rise; the low price elasticity of demand for tin resulted in an increase in total world expenditure on the commodity, thus increasing the profitability of producers. This stimulated extra production, especially from countries like Burma and Peru which were non-ITC members; it also brought a major new producer into the market in the shape of Brazil, which began exploiting huge reserves of tin in the Amazon region. The world supply curve shifted to the right, prices began to drift down. This was resisted by the ITC with restrictions on exports of tin.

During the 1980s, the world demand curve for tin shifted to the left because of world recession together with the development of an alternative in the form of the aluminium can. The ITC then tried to establish a buffer stock; but with demand declining and supply increasing the ITC became a continuous buyer. Unlike the CAP, which is financed by European taxpayers, and whose funds are limited only by the extent to which voters are aware of, and willing to tolerate, a transfer of incomes from themselves to farmers, the funds of the ITC are much more limited, depending on contributions from member-governments and loans. Quite soon the buffer stock ran out of money. Banks and brokers holding collateral on loans in the form of options on tin rushed to sell these to try to recover some of their debts, thus creating the danger of a total collapse of the world tin price. Thus the London Metal Exchange was forced to suspend the market for tin.

The alternative for Brazil would have been to have established a buffer stock to smooth fluctuations in price and supply by buying when prices are low and the commodity abundant and selling when prices are high and there is shortage. Buffer stocks have existed off and on for a range of commodities (wheat, tin, rubber, coffee, sugar, cocoa) since the 1920s, but all large commodity agreements have failed eventually so there is no prominent example to consider. In order to attempt to *stabilise* prices and guarantee availability an organisation is created, such as the International Tin Council (ITC). This organisation's failure is considered in detail in Box 7.1. Its operation is shown in Figure 7.8. The buffer stock manager had a fund contributed by eight producer and 16 consumer nations. His responsibility was to buy stocks in years of abundance, shown by supply curve S_{W2} to keep prices above the 'floor' level P_F. These stocks were stored until a year of scarcity, shown by supply curve S_{W1}. Stocks would then be released to bring the price below the 'ceiling' price P_C. The price levels shown, including an equilibrium price P_E, would be estimated from the manager's knowledge of long term conditions.

It is often suggested that agreements of this sort can raise the incomes of LDCs by counteracting a tendency for their terms of trade to deteriorate, and in the 1960s the United Nations Conference on Trade and Development (UNCTAD) encouraged the establishment of such organisations. However, there has been a tendency for buffer stock managers to run out of the commodity, in which case the price escapes decisively above the ceiling; or to run out of funds (as happened with tin), in which case the price falls through the floor. The commodity price is then left to speculators, who need large fluctuations in price to encourage them to speculate, so disorderly conditions return.

Commodity trade agreements existed to guarantee a stable and satisfactory level of income to producers and stable and satisfactory prices to consumers. An agreement of producers to limit supply without the consumer is a *cartel*. A cartel is an agreement between producers to cooperate in order to fix output and hence prices. The theoretical opposite: an agreement of consumers to boycott a product or the activities of an MNE as yet has no name in economics. However, one may be needed shortly, as *non governmental organisations* (NGOs) have become increasingly important pressure groups in voicing public disquiet over the activities of MNEs. Christian Aid recently forced Reebok and Nike to improve minimum pay and working conditions for the manufacture of trainers in the

Philippines; other pressure groups forced Gap to end shirt production in Salvador, and Pepsico and Burton to withdraw from Myanmar.

FIGURE   7.8
The Buffer Stock

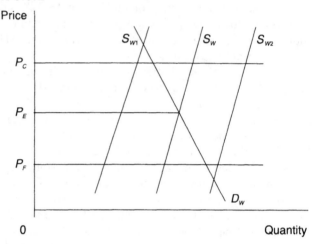

KEY

P_C = Ceiling Price
P_E = Equilibrium Price
P_F = Floor Price
S_{w1} = Year of inadequate Supply
S_{w2} = Year of abundant Supply

Oil has been a special case of supply limitation with the overtones of a cartel. In the early years of the century, the countries of the Persian Gulf and the Far East lacked the capital to exploit their oil reserves, so production rights were negotiated with American and European companies in return for royalties. Competition drove down oil prices (and therefore royalties) in the 1950s so the main exporting countries formed a producers' association – OPEC (the Organisation of Petroleum Exporting Countries) in 1961. Royalty revenues fell only slowly during the next ten years, but by the early 1970s the industrialised world was heavily dependent on cheap crude oil, especially the high quality oils from the Persian Gulf. Following the war between Egypt and Israel in 1973, the Arab members of OPEC led by Saudi Arabia cut back exports to put pressure on Israel's friends, resulting in a quadrupling of the dollar oil price. The process was repeated in 1979, resulting in a further doubling of the oil price. These oil price shocks are of massive importance to our understanding of the world economy in the 1980s and 1990s. Some of the consequences are as follows.

Firstly, the extra revenue royalties were used by the producer companies to complete a process of nationalisation of oil assets begun in the early 1970s. From now on oil would be produced by companies belonging to the producer countries, employing the big oil companies for contract services. Further supply limitations would be possible.

Secondly, the increased royalty revenues were beyond the producer countries' immediate needs for development, so they were deposited in the commercial banks of the developed world. These banks sought borrowers and found a ready market for floating rate debt in the LDCs. When interest rates rose in the early 1980s, the *debt crisis* resulted. (See Chapter 8.)

Thirdly, the extent of dependence on non-renewable energy sources was obvious to all. In the MDCs, concern over resource depletion, and over what price should be paid to conserve the earth's irreplaceable assets, was the start of the environmentalist movement. Ironically, the high prices brought new, hitherto uncompetitive, non-OPEC suppliers such as Britain and Norway into the market, contributing to a steady fall in the real price of oil after 1986.

Lastly, the OPEC countries found that by coordinating restricted supply to the oil market, they could keep the price above normal competitive levels, allowing members to supply less but maintain revenues. This has been seen as a cartel, whose success lasted until 1986, when it became impossible to persuade the members to follow Saudi Arabia's lead any longer. The decline in OPEC's share of the world oil market (for a few months Britain actually produced more oil than Saudi Arabia in the early 1990s) showed the cartel was an ultimate victim of its own success. In practice international cartels such as OPEC cannot be 'outlawed', other than by agreement between sovereign states, but it is not for nothing that within certain countries similar agreements would most definitely be regarded as illegal. In the UK, for example, cartels are subject to legal scrutiny. The EU has more stringent views and the European Commissioner for

Competition is likely to tighten up on this area of producer behaviour as time goes on. The USA has the strictest laws against monopolies and cartels in the MDCs.

Where international commodity agreements aim to stabilise prices – so that over a period of years the average price of the commodity is near to the long-run market price – then there is greater prospect of success than when the aim is to raise prices above the long-term level through cartelisation as OPEC did between 1973 and 1986. The experience of international cartels is that they tend to be unstable; if members 'cheat' on their quotas, or if large producers refuse to join, then they can break up quite easily.

The General Agreement on Tariffs and Trade

The General Agreement on Tariffs and Trade (GATT) was one of three institutions set up in the wake of the Bretton Woods Agreements of 1944 as part of the Anglo-American grand design for post-war economic development (the other two being the IMF and IBRD). Originally intended to be called the International Trade Organisation, to foster free trade in contrast to the beggar-my-neighbour protectionist policies of the 1930s, it was stillborn. GATT was its smaller, voluntary replacement. The GATT agreement was signed in Geneva in 1947 by 23 countries, and its membership steadily grew to well over 100. Finally on January 1st 1995 it was replaced by the World Trade Organisation (WTO), which has taken over the task of encouraging trade liberalisation.

Since the Second World War world trade has increased forty-eight fold in terms of value, and twelve fold in terms of volume. Many economists believe that this remarkable increase has been due, at least in part, to the trade liberalisation which has taken place through the eight 'rounds' of *multinational trade negotiations* (MTNs) under the auspices of GATT. Each was larger and more successful than the last. The first five rounds between 1947 and 1956 discussed tariffs only, but the Kennedy Round (1962–67) introduced discussion of non-tariff barriers, the MFA, and agriculture. The eighth round, the Uruguay Round, started at Punta del Este in 1986 and was completed in 1994, some 4 years late. During the round it is estimated that tariffs among industrialised countries fell from about ten per cent to 3.7 per cent, but the agenda was much wider.

The underlying principles of GATT have not changed since its foundation and will be continued by the World Trade Organisation. GATT favoured *multilateralism*, a term used to refer to trade between more than two countries, without any discrimination against particular countries. The opposite of multilateralism is *bilateralism*, or trade between two countries which necessarily involves discrimination if privileges are given which are denied to other countries. For example, Australia and Malaysia give preferential treatment to each others' products in the home market: Malaysian tin and rubber avoid protectionism in Australia in return for the same concession for Australian wheat in Malaysia. The *most favoured nation* (MFN) rule in Article 1 implies that GATT would approve of the *reciprocity* in this agreement between Australia and Malaysia but that it should be extended to all other GATT members. Signatories to a trade treaty who offer each other favourable trading terms (such as tariff reductions) must then offer them to any other country. Thus the rounds involved across-the-board, multilateral negotiated reductions in tariffs. GATT also favoured transparency – visibility and certainty in trade relations. Permitted departures from these basic principles are action against dumping, and the establishment of free trade areas (see below).

While multilateralism is generally accepted as a 'good thing' which will encourage trade and hence increase economic welfare generally, the LDCs have had suspicions that its effect might be to strengthen the already strong and weaken the already weak. They have been particularly critical of the MFN clause. When UNCTAD was established, following the Prebisch Report in the early 1960s, the 'infant industry' argument was used to support the idea of LDCs being allowed to discriminate against imports of manufactures from the MDCs, and at the same time it was argued that MDCs should discriminate in favour of exports from LDCs. As a result LDCs are, to some extent, exempt from the MFN provisions of GATT. Enthusiasts for further liberalisation would argue that the time will come when LDCs will regard this exemption as a hindrance rather than as a help to their further development; they would point to the success of the newly-industrialised countries of the Pacific, and argue that countries with a policy of aggressively marketing their exports round the world would benefit from MFN status.

The Uruguay Round set up 15 negotiating groups to deal with the new protectionism. Among the important topics were VERs, agriculture, settlement of disputes, *trade related intellectual property rights* (TRIPS), *trade related investment measures* (TRIMS), and services. With 105 nations present, and such a vast agenda, we should not be surprised at the delay in signing, more that it was signed at all !

The background history of international trade in the eight years of negotiation meant that the progress of the Uruguay Round was one of fits and starts. The debt crisis, the collapse of the Soviet Union, the enlargement of the EU and the creation of trade blocs in North and South America and South East Asia raised new questions as the talks proceeded. Two topics of importance to LDCs and development are summarised below:

1. TRIPS consist of the patents, trademarks, copyrights and brands which large companies use to protect the ownership of ideas in MDCs. Microsoft's Windows 95 computer operating system was copied and sold at a fraction of the price of the original product in South East Asia within days of its publication in late 1995. Microsoft had borne the vast development costs and therefore priced it to repay those costs and reward its shareholders, but became so worried at the number of 'pirate' copies that it sent investigators to China (which was not then a member of the WTO) to try to find their sources. Copies of Rolex watches, audio CDs and designer clothes are other common examples. In the early 1990s it was estimated that MDC owners of intellectual property rights were losing $60 billion a year. An implication of this illicit form of technology transfer was that LDCs and former communist countries, where intellectual property rights were weaker, were gaining billions of dollars worth of employment and production. LDCs reluctantly agreed to strengthen their intellectual property laws, with patents to last 20 years with new sectors such as pharmaceuticals included. It was recognised by the MDCs that this would increase the costs of LDCs trying to develop new industries, so a four-year transitional period was granted from January 1995, and an additional five years for the least developed countries, mainly in Africa. By 2004 all LDCs should have brought their intellectual property laws into line with those of the MDCs, the process overseen by the World Intellectual Property Organisation (WIPO) in Geneva.

2. Agriculture was a source of particular friction. Since the 1950s it had been excluded from trade negotiations, and levels of protec-

tionism were particularly high in Japan and Europe. The *Cairns Group*, which included LDC producers as well as Australia and New Zealand, succeeded in getting agriculture on to the agenda, and strong pressure from this group and the USA (itself somewhat protectionist) was put on the EU to reform the Common Agricultural Policy (CAP). In the late stages, the success of the whole round appeared to depend on the EU agreeing to CAP reform, and it had begun the difficult task of weaning farmers away from subsidy.

Globalisation

Internationalisation of trade has been taking place for centuries; economists argue that globalisation is not quite the same thing, and has only been taking place for decades, coinciding with new communication technologies and the liberalisation of money and capital markets.

In many industries there is a 'minimum efficient scale', or a level of output which must be reached before scale economies are sufficient to ensure profitability. In car manufacturing, for example, profit margins on each car are such that in order to stay in the market for the run-of-the-mill family car, producers must manufacture in very large numbers or not at all. Hence there is a trend towards oligopoly, with the world market increasingly becoming dominated by fewer, larger groupings. These groupings are increasingly able to locate specialist plant in different corners of the globe, seeking out lowest-cost locations for each stage of the production process. This particular example helps to explain the general trend towards globalisation.

A simple (and therefore meangingful and useful) definition of 'globalisation', devised by Peter Jay, the BBC's Economics Correspondent, runs along the following lines: 'The ability to produce any good (or service) anywhere in the world, using raw materials, components, capital and technology from anywhere, sell the resulting output anywhere, and place the profits anywhere.'

Global free trade is clearly beneficial to the managers and shareholders of the multinationals, who would like nothing better than to receive profits generated from the economies of scale that would be created if everyone in the world were to drive the same motor car, eat the same hamburger, or wear the same baseball cap.

Some observers believe that globalisation has automatic benefits for the majority of the world's population. Such observers tend to believe in a 'trickle-down' theory of economic distribution. They believe that although globalisation might lead to a more unequal share out of the world production 'cake', it will result in a bigger overall cake and thus benefit poorer sections of world society as well as the better off. Other observers believe that growth of the cake will be insufficient to benefit everyone, and that the haves will take a bigger slice than the have-nots.

The World Bank tends to favour the 'trickle-down' view. They believe that there is a positive correlation between freeing markets and trade and the eradication of poverty in the long term; that there is no evidence that free trade pushes down wages for unskilled workers; and that world growth is the most promising way to reduce poverty in the LDCs. The United Nations Development Programme, on the other hand, is not so sanguine about the benefits of free trade. The view from the UN is that increased global competition does not automatically bring faster growth and development; that in almost all LDCs that have undertaken trade liberalisation unemployment has increased and unskilled wages have fallen; and that growth in the world economy in the forseeable future will be too slow to significantly reduce poverty.

A substantial minority of economists are arguing that protectionism is not always a bad thing, and that protective barriers might actually surround some things that are worth protecting, such as a distinctive culture, or a region which depends on a particular industry for its way of life.

Regionalism and Trading Blocs

Partly in response to the success of the European Union, partly as a reaction to the challenge to the nation-state presented by globalisation, other groups of countries have begun forming themselves into trading blocs. This is contrary to the GATT approach of multilateralism. If North and South America, Africa, and the Asia/Pacific form regional trading groups, then LDCs might find themselves seriously disadvantaged; the arguments advanced against the protectionism of the CAP would apply equally to these other blocs. Essentially, the arguments are two-fold:

1. The export of EU surpluses to LDCs constitutes the 'dumping' of foodstuffs at low prices.
2. Trade barriers deny the LDCs access to markets within the EU.

In the World Development Report of 1986 the World Bank made a stinging attack on the CAP and its other equivalents around the world, and estimated that taxpayers and consumers in OECD countries were paying 100 billion per year in farm support and protection. Paradoxically, only half of this money actually benefited producers, most of the money resulting in the long run in higher land prices or rents. The report argued that artificially high prices not only raised output uneconomically, but subsidised exports while discriminating against imports. Since LDCs often rely on agriculture for 30–40 per cent of GDP this was harming economic development.

Do regional trading blocs increase or decrease world economic welfare and do they accelerate or decelerate the move towards global free trade?

Before answering these questions it is important to distinguish between the different levels of trade cooperation possible within trade blocs. At the simplest level is the *free trade area* (FTA), where a group of countries agree to free trade among themselves but retain their individual external tariffs. Internal frontier checks are still necessary to stop trade re-routing itself over the lowest external barrier in the bloc. Next, in order of economic integration, comes the *Customs Union*, which is an FTA with a Common External Tariff. Members agree a suitable level of protectionism for all, and can move towards the common administration of external trade. Finally, the *Common Market* is a Customs Union which also allows the free movement of factors of production between members.

The European Union announced this third stage in 1992, but the abolition of complex internal regulations to allow completely free migration of capital and labour continues. The EU has 15 member states (from January 1995) plus extra associated states such as Norway and Iceland which enjoy FTA status forming the *European Economic Area*. The proposed full membership of the Vizegrad Four (Poland, Hungary, the Czech Republic and Slovakia) necessarily takes many years since the EU has already reached the third level of integration and is proposing a fourth in the form of a *single European currency*. Thus the EU is attempting to widen and deepen itself as a trade bloc at the same time. The *North American Free Trade Area*

BOX 7.2

Case Study: The North American Free Trade Area and Labour

The NAFTA Agreement was signed in 1992 and became effective in January 1994. It created free trade in goods and capital but not freedom of movement of people. Four categories of temporary migrant were allowed greater freedom of movement: workers needing training in another country, traders and investors, international business people, and employees transferred within their firms from one NAFTA country to another.

While NAFTA could increase short-run pressures to migrate from Mexico to the USA, in the long run Mexico's development should reduce the incentive to emigrate. Already 3000 *maquiladoras* (Mexican factories doing assembly work for the US car, textile, furniture and electronics industries) have appeared close to the border.

An example of how development can contain migration is to be found in the production of berries in Mexico. Berrymex, a Californian company has leased farmland and placed contracts with Mexican farmers, and under NAFTA's reinforced protection of intellectual property rights, has allowed cultivation of its patented raspberry plants. Skilled Mexican farm workers, who had previously migrated to the USA to look for seasonal work now volunteered for Berrymex jobs out of a desire to return home. Although the wages were lower, it reduced the strain of six months of separation from families and the cost of running two homes.

Trade creation under NAFTA is illustrated by the trade in avocados. Since 1914 Mexican avocados have been banned from the US for health reasons, though this may be partly lifted in November 1997. But Mission Produce of California has already taken advantage of the liberalisation of farm trade by investing in Mexico. In 1996, the company contracted 500 Mexican growers who delivered 20 000 tons of avocados to the company, which exported them to Europe and Japan. Mission would be willing to invest more if Mexico's foreign investment laws were relaxed further, an indication that trade cooperation creates pressures for further integration.

SOURCE   *OECD Observer* no. 192, February 1995.

(NAFTA) is at the first level of integration and considering widening itself at that level rather than deepening itself as in Europe. *MERCO-SUR* and *ASEAN* are at the early stages of FTA status, and many more proposed trade blocs are in the air in the late 1990s. Clearly regional trade blocs are popular and believed to be beneficial.

Returning to the question of whether they promote economic welfare, it all depends on the difference between *trade creation* (the ability of freer trading arrangements to generate new output) and *trade diversion* (the tendency for trading blocs to redistribute existing output to different trading partners rather than to increase the total amount of output).

A trade bloc improves global welfare only if it creates more trade than it diverts. If neighbouring countries already trade significantly with each other, the removal of tariffs will probably increase the gains from specialisation and trade, unless their new common tariff wall creates a barrier to more efficiently produced imports from non FTA countries. However, neighbouring countries do not necessarily have big trade flows with each other: African countries, for instance export 95 per cent of their goods to countries outside Africa.

Trade creation and trade diversion can be illustrated as in Figure 7.9 which shows the market for washing machines in three cases: an imaginary Britain outside the EU; Britain inside the EU with a rival producing country, Italy; and Britain in Adam Smith's dream world of universal free trade.

The diagram incorporates three supply curves for washing machines: British output is shown by the curve S_{UK}, trade bloc output is shown by the curve S_{UK+IT}, and world output is shown by the now familiar horizontal supply curve S_W. The trade creation effects of Britain joining the EU with Italy can be seen in the fall in price of washing machines from P_{UK} to P_{UK+IT} and the increase in the size of the market from Q_1 to Q_2. The triangle *EAB* shows the trade creation effect. By maintaining a Common External Tariff the gains from the free trade world are denied to the citizens of the EU: these would be a further fall in price to P_W and an extension of the market to Q_3. Thus the trade diversion effect is represented by the triangle FBC.

Trading blocs between MDCs are likely to be successful, for example one academic report claimed that EU GDP was already 5.9 per cent larger in 1981 than it would have been without the existence of the organisation. But this implies a net gain in trade creation over trade diversion, and the trade diversion may well have been at the

FIGURE 7.9
Trade Creation and Trade Diversion

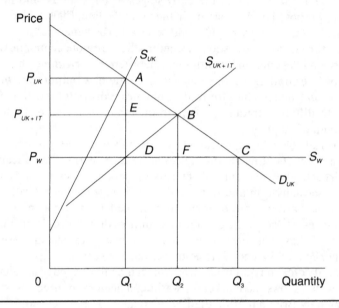

KEY

	UK Trades Alone	In Trade Bloc with Italy	Free Trade World
Price, Quantity	P_{UK}, Q_1	P_{UK+IT}, Q_2	P_W, Q_3
Trade Creation	–	EAB	DAC
Trade Diversion	DAC	FBC	–

expense of LDCs which were part of the former trading and political empires of France and Britain. The Lomé Conventions and the preservation of the CFA zone are recognitions of this.

Trading blocs between LDCs are unlikely to yield large welfare gains; however, a bloc including LDCs and large MDCs (such as a link between North and South America) could have benefits, since it would guarantee access to a large market and thus encourage economies of scale. The cheap labour of the LDC would find itself in the same regional trading bloc as the cheap capital of the MDC. Here the relationship between the USA and Mexico within NAFTA since January 1994 is of particular interest. In a long-awaited report in July 1997, the US government pointed to an increase in US exports to Mexico of 37 per cent over three years, notwithstanding the appearance of a Mexican trade surplus with the USA of $16 billion. US officials claim NAFTA as an important factor moving Mexico towards prosperity, and that this justifies the opening of trade negotiations with Chile and other Latin American and Asian countries. The trade creation effect can be seen most clearly in textiles: between 1993 and 1996, Mexico's textile exports to the USA tripled to $4.2 billion, Canada's clothing and textile exports to the USA doubled to $2 billion, and the USA's textile exports to Canada grew 39 per cent to $2.7 billion and to Mexico by 79 per cent to $2.8 billion.

Do regional trading blocs provide a better route towards global free trade than multilateral negotiations such as the Uruguay Round? It could be argued that negotiations between three or four FTAs would be quicker and more likely to lead to agreement on trade liberalisation than negotiating rounds with over 100 participants. On the other hand, the experience of the EU is that agreement between FTA members is often so precariously based on fine adjustments and compromises, that there is little or no room for manoeuvre left when it comes to negotiate with outsiders. Large, powerful blocs might well be tempted to protect their big home markets from competition from outside. A good test of whether regional deals encourage the liberalisation of trade is to ask whether the bloc is open to new members. If so, then any country willing to lower its trade barriers on the same terms as the agreement's existing parties would be offered preferential trade terms in return, and so the frontiers of liberal trade would be continuously pushed outwards. In reality, most trading blocs tend to be exclusive clubs, with their minds closed to the idea of allowing outsiders to gain membership.

There is talk of the EU being likely to expand to some Eastern European countries; and it is possible that Latin American countries could join NAFTA. Such expansion could actually be counterproductive if fears of being shut out of these two groups cause Asian countries to set up an FTA of their own. ASEAN already has plans to reduce tariffs on nearly all intra-ASEAN trade to below 5 per cent by 2003, and to remove most non-tariff barriers to imports. Much depends on the future of the World Trade Organisation; if it fails, members might fall back on FTAs which then could turn out to be anything but a stepping stone towards global free trade.

On the other hand, it can be argued that regional blocs are benef-icial – particularly to their less advantaged citizens – if they help to ameliorate the harsher effects of globalisation. If, for instance, right-wing governments in Europe were to assert their nationalism and oppose Europe-wide social legislation, then multinationals might be given free reign to drive down wages, worsen working conditions, and pollute the environment. One way of viewing 'global development' is in terms of 'de-pauperisation', and it can be argued that groups of countries need to act in concert in order to strive for this.

The Debt Crisis

8

How can international trade be paid for? Why are LDCs in debt? Why did Latin America suffer a 'lost decade' after 1982? Why was Africa's income per head no higher in 1990 than in the 1960s? Is 'aid' likely to improve the position of LDCs?

Currency and Exchange Rates

International trade does not take place between nations but between individuals and organisations within those nations. When Mexico imports machine parts from the USA, what is really meant is that a Mexican business has purchased machine parts from an American one. To pay for these imported goods, the Mexican firm has to obtain US dollars. This convention of paying for imports in the currency of the producing country means that most international trade is impossible without some system of currency exchange rates. There are exceptions: some trade is done in barter, and some in dominant 'hard' currencies that are more acceptable than local weak ones. Oil is always denominated in US dollars throughout the world.

The international exchange rate system has three general problems associated with it:

1. the liquidity problem;
2. the adjustment problem;
3. the confidence problem.

How do these problems particularly relate to development?

The liquidity problem

For international trade to take place, there must be international liquidity to pay for that trade. Unfortunately, there is no such thing as a world currency. Because of its special qualities as a precious metal, gold is perhaps the nearest thing that we have to a generally acceptable international medium of exchange, though its importance has declined in the last twenty years and reserves to back currencies have been allowed to run down. For example, Australia sold two-thirds of its gold reserves in July 1997. As a substitute for gold, 'hard' currencies such as the Dollar, Yen and German Mark with relatively stable exchange rates have been used. Some of these currencies have at times been used as international reserves – used not just in their own countries but traded internationally and held by foreign governments and international organisations as part of their reserves. The problem with hard currencies is that their degree of relative hardness can vary from time to time due to large short-run and long-run fluctuations in exchange rates. In the year from August 1996 the US Dollar and the British Pound have appreciated by over 25 per cent against the Japanese Yen and German Mark. This short-run fluctuation is in marked contrast to long-run trends: the Pound lost an average of five per cent a year in its exchange rate with the German Mark from 1949 to 1996. Furthermore, the supply of hard currencies alone has not increased rapidly enough to match the increase in international trade. The currencies of the LDCs have shown a strong tendency to lose value against the hard currencies, unless protected by special arrangements such as the French CFA zone. This fixed link between the French Franc and former colonies was stable for many years until a 50 per cent devaluation in 1994.

Fixed exchange systems, where exchange rates remain unchanged for long periods, provide a good climate for those involved in international trade. Export revenues and import bills can be predicted. Even more certainty could come from a global currency. At the UN Monetary and Financial Conference at Bretton Woods in 1944, so unpleasant was the memory of the 1930s floating rates, retaliatory protectionism and lack of cooperation that work began to encourage free trade, stable exchange rates, and a multilateral payments system between members. The result was the IMF, financed by a 'quota' from each member country, linked to that country's importance in world trade. At the Conference, the British economist Keynes proposed the creation of an international currency called 'Bancor', but it was not until 1969 that the IMF began to tackle the liquidity problem in this manner, when it established a system of 'Special Drawing Rights' (SDR). An SDR is valued in terms of a 'basket' of major currencies. Every two years an allocation of SDRs is decided upon by the IMF and they are distributed to members in proportion to their IMF quotas. Over the years, the SDR has gradually become more acceptable, and many commercial banks will accept deposits in SDRs as an alternative to national currencies. While the SDR has helped to finance an increase in world trade, it is still very far short of being a true international currency. Countries which do not belong to the IMF, or whose currencies are 'soft' rather than hard, often find that they have to resort to 'barter' in order to take part in inter-national trade. This was particularly true of the Soviet planned economies. Poland, for example bartered hams and skis for imports in the early 1980s. Barter is a far less convenient and efficient means than money as an exchange medium, and countries relying on barter can expect to have to wait for a dual coincidence of wants, so the process of economic development is significantly slowed down.

The adjustment problem

In 1973 the Bretton Woods system of fixed exchange rates administered by the IMF was abandoned in favour of floating exchange rates. Two main arguments were put forward to support this change. *Firstly*, with floating there is a reduced risk of imported inflation of the type associated with once-and-for-all devaluations. Devaluations had become rather disorderly, surrounded by unpreventable speculation while the country in 'fundamental disequilibrium' waited for the IMF to decide the case. Under floating, a deficit country would automatically experience a gradual depreciation of its currency, which would correct the deficit. *Secondly*, governments would be freed from the need to worry about balance of payments problems and gearing domestic monetary and fiscal policy to solve them; instead, they could concentrate on internal monetary and budgetary policies, and leave the exchange rate to adjust itself and the balance of payments accordingly.

In practice, such advantages have not fully materialised. Shortly after the abandonment of Bretton Woods, the international economy experienced a series of 'exogenous shocks', such as the oil price increases of 1973 and 1979, and the rise of the debt problem of the LDCs. These disturbances caused balance of payments difficulties on a scale which many countries had never previously experienced. They also gave the IMF a new role as a lender and fixer of these difficulties through the use of 'structural adjustment programmes'. During the 1980s, the abandoning of exchange controls and the deliberate deregulation of financial markets in the larger industrial countries greatly increased the mobility of capital between countries. Differences in exchange rates began to much more closely reflect differences in interest rates, as 'hot money' capital flows were transferred between banks in different countries. Most countries therefore adopted a system of 'managed' exchange rates or 'dirty floating', where governments attempted to intervene on the financial markets to smooth exchange rate fluctuations.

Some groups of countries attempted to fix exchange rates between themselves, while floating as a whole against other world currencies (the Exchange Rate Mechanism (ERM) of the EU, for example), while some countries chose to attach themselves to a chosen hard currency (the Bahrain dinar, for instance, is one of about 30 currencies which are pegged to the US dollar). The proposed introduction of the Euro for qualifying members of the EU from January 1999 is meant to fuse monetary policy across large areas of the single market.

When the terms of trade (see Chapter 5) of LDCs tend to deteriorate, there is a tendency for there to be trade deficits and thus downward pressure on the exchange rates of LDCs against the currencies of MDCs. This leads to imported inflation, and further lost competitiveness and exchange rate depreciation. These relationships are explained in Figure 5.1. An alternative explanation of how domestic inflation leads to exchange rate depreciation is found in the Theory of *Purchasing Power Parity* (PPP). This theory suggests that floating exchange rates between countries adjust themselves until the price of a given basket of goods is the same in both. If two countries both export coffee and country A suffers 10 per cent inflation and country B has zero inflation, the first country's exchange rate will depreciate by the rate of inflation so that its coffee exports remain competitive in third country markets. Thus country A's depreciation will be equal to the excess of its inflation over country B's. It follows that LDC currencies' tendency to depreciate will be equal to the excess of their inflation over world inflation.

The confidence problem

It is often suggested that exchange rate volatility increases uncertainty and reduces business confidence. It makes it more difficult for firms to estimate costs and revenues in advance, and thus harms world trade. The LDCs were particularly fearful of the introduction of floating exchange rates because of the possibility of large currency fluctuations. Most primary products are sold on world markets in hard currencies, and so the balance of payments of the LDCs supplying them can be unexpectedly damaged by sudden currency adjustments. Floating exchange rates might also make it more difficult for LDCs to repay their international debts. It has been argued by some economists that in order to try to reduce uncertainty, floating exchange rates might encourage LDCs to adopt increased protectionism. However, studies by the IMF have suggested that floating exchange rates have had a less harmful effect on LDCs than other factors, including the deflationary policies of MDCs which have involved high world interest rates, and the barriers to trade erected by some of the international arrangements of the MDCs such as the EU's Common Agricultural Policy.

International Saving, Investing and Borrowing

One way of defining the term LDC is along the lines suggested by W.W. Rostow: as a country which has not yet reached a stage of growth where its national income creates enough saving to finance investment for further growth. Rostow suggested that to achieve take-off into self-sustaining growth, countries have to raise the rate of effective savings and investment from under 5 per cent to ten per cent or more. We have already referred to the 'development trap', which describes a cycle of poverty where low income leads to low saving, low saving leads to low investment, and low investment leads in turn to low income. But Rostow's model applies to self-starters: if a country wishes to invest more than it saves, then it can look beyond its borders for flows of money. These flows can come in three main forms:

1. foreign direct investment (FDI);
2. borrowing;
3. aid.

Foreign direct investment

In recent years foreign direct investment (FDI) has increased dramat-ically. In 1985 it was $47 billion, in 1989 $132 billion, and in 1994 $225 billion. Most of this was between MDCs but during the period 1990 to 1995 the flow to LDCs quadrupled to over $90 billion. This looks like good news: LDCs claim a much larger percentage of total FDI than they did at the beginning of the decade and earlier. In the second half of the 1980s the LDCs share of total FDI had been falling from 25 per cent towards 15 per cent, but it has grown to nearly 40 per cent by the mid 1990s. However, examination of the particular countries receiv-ing FDI reveals some disturbing trends. In 1995 all of sub-Saharan Af-rica (excluding South Africa) received less than $2.2 billion, that is 2.4 per cent of the total going to LDCs. This amount is less than that re-ceived by Chile alone, and a considerable reduction on the previous year. In contrast 59 per cent went to the East Asia and Pacific region and 20 per cent to Latin America and the Caribbean.

What explains the way FDI is distributed? Not all governments wel-come direct investment from foreign firms, and may deter them by out-right rejection or by setting conditions such as local content agreements or profit retention agreements. This is a form of protectionism, designed to shield local producers from more efficient foreign-owned business. Although India's change to outward orientation has been quite marked since the IMFs intervention in 1991, it rejected a ma-jor FDI proposal in 1995 for a power station in Maharashtra state. Local politicians spoke of preventing foreign efforts to corrupt and dominate India, though in reality it was more to do with nationalist opposition to a Texan gas company making good profits from selling electricity to Indians. This form of protectionism, regulating FDI, was one of the hot-test topics at the WTO's conference at Singapore in December 1996.

Secondly, FDI will not be offered to countries where the business community has a perception that there is risk to its activities. The opening up of formerly centrally planned economies in the 1990s has made them much lower risk propositions, while the tragic political upheavals of central Africa have caused the opposite effect. For ex-ample, in 1994 Hungary attracted $1.1 billion of FDI (equivalent to $111 per head of population). The private sector branch of the World Bank, the International Finance Corporation (IFC) is responsible for supporting most FDI in the poorest countries of Africa, but it has been forced to write off its earlier loans to Zaire, with the result that no more were made between 1992 and 1996. According to *The Economist* a country considered 'high risk' by the IFC would have a weak currency, exchange controls, a weak private sector, small domestic markets, stifling bureaucracy, political instability, uncertain legal systems and corruption. Africa has a larger share of such countries than anywhere else.

If the distribution of FDI is influenced by risk and willingness to accept, it is not surprising that most of it consists of flows between MDCs. Wales, for example, has the highest concentration of Japanese firms outside Japan itself. This inward investment has been encouraged by the UK government as a means of reducing unemployment, and has been welcomed by Japanese and American enterprise as providing a production base inside the Common External Tariff of the EU with its 340 million consumers. Some German firms have also relocated to Wales to take advantage of cheaper labour, with the surprising result that manufacturing has climbed to 31 per cent of Welsh GDP compared with only 21 per cent for the whole of Britain. The issue now facing the LDCs is whether they can increase their share of FDI flows, and whether politically difficult decisions, such as the abandonment of protectionism for 'infant industries' and the acceptance of free market philosophies towards goods, labour, and social services are adequately repaid by the economic benefits of playing a fuller part in international production.

Borrowing from international institutions

Mention has already been made of the role of the IMF in exchange rate adjustment. It also acts as a lending institution. IMF lending is not solely concerned with LDCs, but with any member country, and was originally intended to overcome temporary balance of payments difficulties. But in the 1970s and 1980s, due to the end of Bretton Woods, the oil price rise, and the problems of LDC debt (see below), the amount and the role of IMF lending was extended. (For example, see Box 8.1.) The *conditionality* of this lending is sometimes controversial because fund loans are accompanied by a programme of measures agreed with the recipient country. Low income countries have access to earmarked IMF funds on low rates of interest with long repayment terms.

BOX 8.1

IMF Programmes: An Example

Fund facilities

15-month stand-by arrangement (SBA) agreed for SDR 590 million (about $843 million) to support economic reform programme. Purchases (or drawings) to be made in 5 instalments. Repurchases (or repayments) made over 3 years.

Macro-economic objectives

Over programme period, to achieve:

- real economic growth rate of about 5 per cent;
- reduction in inflation from 20 per cent to 5 per cent; and
- sizeable balance-of-payments surplus.

Structural and financial reforms

Reforms are intended to liberalise the economy, shifting from centralised system to a market determined environment. Key elements include:

- liberalisation of exchange system, accompanied by an appropriate exchange rate policy and elimination of external payment arrears;
- lifting of price controls;
- liberalisation of interest rates and removal of sectoral credit controls;
- strengthening of domestic banking system;
- reform of state enterprises including privatisation; and
- tax reform to increase incentives.

Over 50 countries now have IMF lending programmes, and the expansion of lending together with conditionality, mean that the IMF has a great deal of influence over economic policies all over the world, particularly in the LDCs, where a Fund programme is often seen as a seal of approval, giving access to further investment from other international organisations, and from private sector banks and multinational enterprises.

The International Bank for Reconstruction and Development (IBRD) was set up at the same time as the IMF, and works closely with that institution. The IBRD, together with the International Development Association (IDA), the International Finance Corporation (IFC), and the Multilateral Investment Guarantee Agency (MIGA) are collectively referred to as the 'World Bank'.

The IBRD raises money by selling bonds on the world market, and makes loans either direct to national governments or increasingly to business enterprises if the national government acts as guarantor. It lends for investment projects, such as a dam or a road, or to support economic reform either generally or in a particular sector. The bank normally lends to better-off LDCs (defined as those having a per capita GDP of $740–4300); in the year to June 1996 its total lending to LDCs was $21.4 billion. Most lending is at near-commercial rates, but about a third is at subsidised rates through the IDA, which specialises in *concessional* (low interest) loans for large-scale infrastructure projects. It lends at low rates of interest to poorer LDCs (defined as those having per capita GDP of less than $760). These are also known as *soft loans*.

The IFC seeks to increase the involvement of the private sector in international investment, and as well as lending it might take an equity stake in an investment project. Where successful, it is no longer needed, as some companies it has helped have grown large enough to raise money in private markets themselves. Over half its investment goes to Newly Industrialising Countries like Brazil and Mexico, but it is trying to diversify into poorer countries' emerging capital markets and smaller enterprises. The MIGA provides insurance cover against political risk and hence encourages private sector direct investment in some of the less stable corners of the world. In 1995 it insured about $500 million dollars worth of new projects, and has a total portfolio of $2 billion.

Since the early 1980s, many World Bank loans, in similar fashion to IMF loans, have been made conditional on the recipient country adopting certain economic policies known as 'structural adjustment', mainly directed towards the encouragement of private enterprise and removal of trade barriers. The IMF and the World Bank are truly international institutions, and loans from them are referred to as *multilateral borrowing.* The forty most heavily indebted countries in the world owe about a fifth of their total debt to multilateral institutions, but since they are always the first to be paid, they receive a much larger share of the debt interest and repayments actually made. (For examples, see Box 8.2.)

Borrowing from banks: the LDC debt problem

Another kind of debt is commercial debt, so called because it was raised from private commercial banks in the MDCs. The debt crisis of the 1980s was largely caused by the expansion of commercial debt, and can now be considered an historical event with powerful lessons to be drawn from it. During the late 1970s and early 1980s it became clear that a number of LDCs, particularly in Latin America, were no longer able to maintain *debt servicing*: in other words, they were unable to repay either the capital sum borrowed or the interest payments. This problem of LDC debt reflects a certain amount of imprudence by the commercial banks, who reacted to the deregulation of financial markets over-enthusiastically to say the least. Also, OPEC petro-dollars were burning holes in their collective pockets.

In some cases, money was lent to finance projects with little chance of producing income-generating goods and services, simply because they were poor business projects whose future profitability had not been properly appraised; in other cases the money was not invested for business purposes at all, but dissipated on military expenditure, either for possible use against a potentially unfriendly neighbouring country, or even more probably for use by dictators against their own citizens. Commercial banks were more eager to lend than they were to check the income-generating viability of the schemes supported.

In 1982 Mexico announced that it could no longer service its external debt. Similar news from Brazil (1987) and Argentina came soon afterwards. Major banks began to write off billions of dollars from their company accounts due to non-repayment of loans to Latin America: the LDC debt crisis had begun. Measuring the extent of indebtedness is difficult, but a good benchmark is that any country with outstanding debts worth more than 200 per cent of the value of its exports is in difficulty. An alternative would be that any country spending over 40 per cent of its export revenues on debt servicing in any year has similar difficulties. In 1986 the seventeen most heavily indebted countries had net external indebtedness of over 380 per cent of exports. The situation was complicated by *capital flight*, private capital which sped out of the LDCs and into foreign bank accounts when the debt crisis broke, of over $100 billion from 19 debtor countries between 1984 and 1987.

BOX 8.2

Examples of World Bank Loans

Project-related loan

The International Development Association (IDA) will make available a credit of SDR40.5 million ($55 million) to rebuild and maintain roads in fertile farming areas of the recipient country.

Agriculture is the mainstay of the country's economy, providing about half its gross domestic product. Improving rural roads will help boost agriculture production by giving farmers better access to markets and increasing mobility and economic opportunities for the rural poor.

The aim of the project is to help restore 2500 kilometres of feeder roads in areas where the potential for increasing agricultural production is high. About 1000 kilometres of feeder roads will be upgraded using labour-intensive methods, creating employment and increasing incomes for people living in rural areas.

The project includes an effort to sell or lease bicycles, trailers and carts to farmers who will use these vehicles to bring goods to market or to carry out other tasks, such as carrying water. This part of the project will be carried out by non-governmental organisations and cooperatives.

The government will launch a compaign to encourage women to boost their incomes by participating in food rehabilitation and maintenance programmes. Villagers will also be encouraged to plant fruit trees along roads to help prevent soil erosion, produce fuelwood, and further boost incomes through the production of fruit.

BOX 8.2   *(contd.)*

Structural adjustment loan

The recipient country started the implementation of a structural adjustment programme in 1991 with the aim of laying the foundation for faster economic growth. The World Bank approved earlier this year a $125 million loan and the IDA approved a credit of SDR35.9 million ($50 million) in support of the programme.

The challenge facing the recipient country is to achieve more rapid and sustainable growth so as to maintain social advances made during the last decade. The economic reform programme will improve the climate for private investment and exports and create more jobs. Key reforms being implemented under the programme include: cutting the fiscal deficit drastically by 1994, mainly by reducing the deficits of parastatal enterprises and reducing civil service employment; liberalising trade to provide access to capital goods needed to expand investment, introducing a market system for allocating foreign exchange, and lifting import restrictions on all goods by 1995; and increasing domestic competition by removing controls on investment, prices and wages.

Under the adjustment programme, economic growth is expected to rise from 3.4 per cent during the 1980s to 5 per cent by 1995. A projected 100 000 jobs will be created annually over the next five years, and investment as a share of gross domestic product is projected to rise from less than 20 per cent during the 1980s to about 25 per cent this year.

SOURCE   Bank of England, *Economic Briefing*, September 1992.

During the later 1980s negotiations took place to re-schedule these debts, that is to pay them over longer periods of time with reduced rates of interest. These negotiations culminated in the Brady Plan, put forward at a meeting of the Bretton Woods Committee in March 1989 by James Brady, the US Secretary for the Treasury. This plan proposed case-by-case voluntary debt-reduction by the commercial banks, with the IMF and World Bank offering resources to countries with 'viable' economic programmes. Ingenious measures were found to reduce the size and shift the ownership of debts, where the original lenders were paid off a proportion of what was owed in return for transferring the now reduced debt to new owners. The IMF, World Bank, Inter-

American Development Bank and the Japanese government provided collateral to help 18 Brady Plan agreements by 1994. These agreements included $61 billion of debt forgiveness. By 1993 the debt to export percentage had fallen to 225 per cent for the seventeen most indebted countries. The worst of the crisis was over and, at least for Latin America, FDI and other flows began to revive after a 'lost decade'.

However, the crisis was not over for Africa. Much present day African indebtedness originated in the 1980s when multilateral organisations and governments tried to help African countries to cope with rising interest rates, deteriorating terms of trade and existing commercial debt. 32 low income countries, nearly all in Africa, owed $230 billion at the end of 1993, and although this is only 15 per cent of total LDC debt, it was four times as large as their exports. Not much of this debt is commercial debt, but perhaps half is *bilateral* – between two countries only – for example between former French colonies in West Africa and France. Recent discussions in the World Bank have focused on methods of reducing the share of repayments to multilateral agencies like themselves and the IMF.

In many cases, the debt crisis of LDCs reflected unforeseen changes in the economic environment for both lender and borrower. Loans were taken out by oil exporters like Mexico and Venezuela when oil was riding high in the late 1970s at over $40 a barrel, but in 1986 the price collapsed to below $30 a barrel. In the late 1970s, the exports and real incomes of LDCs as a whole were rising at an annual rate of around 10 per cent; but due to world recession they were declining in real terms in the early 1980s. When Argentina's inflation rate rose from 30 per cent to 3000 per cent per year, and when interest rates in Brazil and Chile rose from 10 per cent to 20 per cent, debts became that much more 'difficult to' service. From 1980 to 1982, the export earnings of all LDCs fell by $80 billion or 15 per cent, while their annual interest rate bill rose from $31 billion to $46 billion, an increase of 48 per cent. The LDCs now proved to be casualties of the adoption of new right-wing monetarist policies in Britain and the USA from 1980. As the rate of interest became the central weapon of domestic macroeconomic management under the Thatcher and Reagan governments in the early 1980s, floating-rate debt taken out by LDCs experienced a virtual doubling of interest rates between 1978 and 1983. Where countries were unable to service their debts due to rising interest rates, they borrowed more and more in passive debt accumulation. Thus the debt crisis was to some extent a result of the experiment with monetarism.

Ten years after Mexico's dramatic announcement *The Economist* newspaper carried an article by a prominent banker describing the LDC debt crisis as the 'The disaster that didn't happen'. This might be an accurate description from the point of view of the major banks, since they have managed to survive the decade without one of their number failing due to LDC debt difficulties; however it is arguable whether this view would be shared by citizens of an LDC displaced from their land by an IMF inspired programme to produce cash crops. The appropriateness of IMF free-market ideology has yet to be fully debated, and this debate has to take place not only in Latin America, but in Africa, Asia, and Eastern Europe. Ramifications of the debt crisis can also be seen from an environmental viewpoint, when assets with a global significance, such as South American rain forests, are being cleared to produce grazing for beef cattle. As mentioned earlier, the prudent servicing of external debt involves the creation of income-generating assets. This 'monetarisation' of economic life should not involve the liquidation of non-renewable resources with long-term global environmental consequences in order to overcome a short-term local problem.

Types of aid

The word 'aid' perhaps carries suggestions of charity, but in fact covers a large number of different ways in which money and resources are given by one country to another without expecting full repayment. At one extreme is *grant aid*, where money, food aid or emergency relief are given as a gift with no repayments of any kind expected. A large amount of aid is not sent to LDCs as a gift, but in the form of loans at below-market rates of interest, known as *soft loans*. This contains a grant aid element, which can be calculated by subtracting the expected repayments from those that would obtain in commercial markets, at a suitable discount rate. Thus in broad terms, aid can be regarded as almost any administered transfer of resources from MDCs to LDCs, aimed at encouraging economic growth.

Aid can be *official*, in which case it is administered by governments or government agencies, or it can be unofficial, in which case it is administered by a non-governmental body such as a charity. A great deal of official aid is *tied aid*, which means that the recipient country has to agree to buy goods or services from the donor. In recent years, there has been an increasing tendency for aid to take the form of

BOX 8.3

The Debt Boomerangs

ENVIRONMENT

Debt-induced poverty causes Third World people to exploit natural resources in the most profitable and least sustainable way, which causes an increase in global warming and a depletion of genetic bio-diversity. This ultimately harms the North too.

UNEMPLOYMENT

Exports from rich countries to the Third World would be much higher if those countries were not strapped by debt, and this would stimulate manufacturing and employment in the North. The loss of jobs caused by 'lost exports' is estimated to account for one-fifth of total US unemployment.

DRUGS

The illegal drugs trade is the major earner for heavily indebted countries like Peru, Bolivia and Columbia. The social and economic costs of the drug-consuming boom in the North is phenomenal – $60 bn a year in the USA alone.

IMMIGRATION

The International Labour Organisation estimates that there are about 100 million legal or illegal immigrants and refugees in the world today. Many go to the richer countries of the North to fliee poverty and the effects of IMF-imposed economic policies.

TAXES

Governments in the North have used their taxpayers' money to give banks tax concessions so that they can write off 'bad debts' from Third World countries. But in most cases this has not reduced the actual debts of poor countries. By 1991 UK banks had gained from tax credits for more than half their exposure. The eventual total relief will amount to $8.5 bn

CONFLICT

Debt creates social unrest and war. Iraq invaded Kuwait in 1990 largely in retaliation for the latter's insistence that Saddam's regime repay a $12 bn loan.

SOURCE   Susan George in *The New Internationalist*, May 1993.

mixed credits, which involves MDCs lending LDCs money for the purchase of MDC exports at below-market prices (in effect, a mixture of loan and export subsidy). Mixed credits usually find their way to the better-off LDCs. Many of the flows of money, goods, services, and specialist advice from MDCs to LDCs serve political or military purposes which have little to do with poor people. *Bilateral aid* (from one country to another) tends to follow pathways that are historical, political or cultural in origin: the UK sending aid to former colonies, for example, or OPEC members making donations to other Arab countries. The result is that 40 per cent of these funds flow to countries containing only 20 per cent of the world's poor people. *Multilateral aid* involves the giving of aid to international aid agencies who then decide where need is greatest. As official aid has become more politicised, given with strings attached, and increasingly in the form of loans rather than grants, so there has been a growth in aid from voluntary multilateral aid agencies, such as Oxfam, Cafod, Save the Children and Band Aid. More UK schoolchildren are aware of the work of Comic Relief than have even heard of the World Bank. In 1988, of the $55 billion of bilateral foreign aid flows, some $6 billion came from voluntary efforts, and this proportion is growing rapidly. These groups have the advantage of being non-ideological, widely trusted (often more trusted than governments) and generally targeting their funds carefully towards lasting self-help projects that help the very poorest.

Aid and controversy

Foreign aid has always been the subject of controversy. Critics do not have to search very hard to find evidence that it is often misdirected, badly administered, or even used corruptly. Maladministration is illustrated by the building in April 1993 of the European Bank for Reconstruction and Development (EBRD), which was set up to channel funds into the restructuring of Eastern Europe. It was criticised because during its first year of operation it had given $156 million in investment capital and loans, but spent twice that amount on administrative costs (including the use of private jets) and the refurbishment of its headquarters in London, (including $1.5 million spent on fitting out the entrance lobby with marble from Tuscany). When questioned, EBRD officials agreed that a more cost-conscious policy was necessary, and were quoted as saying that the bank was intended to be a 'profit-making entity answerable to its shareholders, rather than an aid giver'; the implication being that such behaviour is intolerable for a business enterprise, but only to be expected from an aid body.

Tied aid is always a matter of controversy. In 1988 while negotiating a £1.3 billion export order for Hawk trainer aircraft to Malaysia, the British government linked a promise of aid in the form of the £234 million Pergau Dam. Despite attempts to keep this secret, spending the aid budget to secure arms exports was subsequently ruled illegal in the high court and considered economically unsound by a senior civil servant in the Overseas Development Administration. The costs of the dam have climbed subsequently to over £800 million.

Apart from arguing that aid is ineffective in practice, it is also possible to object to it as a matter of principle. There are two lines of argument here, one from the political 'left', and one from the 'right'.

From the left it is argued that aid smacks of charity, and that poor countries do not need money but the ability to create wealth for themselves. *Dependency theory* suggests that aid perpetuates the dependence of countries at the periphery and the dominance of those at the centre. On the other hand it can be argued from the same region of the political spectrum that the ex-colonial powers should repay some of the wealth they have taken from their former colonies, or that there is a moral duty to recognise the interdependence of humanity, and aid relationships are a good way of fostering political allies and friendships.

From the right come suggestions that aid leads to increased government intervention, distorts markets, backs inefficient investment projects and has the effect of crowding out private capital; counter-arguments would include the suggestion that aid makes good business sense for the donor countries, as increased productivity in the LDCs will generate incomes that create larger markets for goods and services produced in the MDCs. Right-wing governments intending to cut their aid budgets often argue sceptically that aid supports bad governments and allows them to continue the pursuit of the wrong policies. Kenya and Malawi were considered examples of this in the 1980s.

The *World Development Report* of 1986 claimed that aid in the narrow sense of gifts, particularly food aid, was only a limited success. It provides a convenient way for some countries, such as EU members, to dispose of their surpluses, which do not always match the dietary needs of the recipients, and the resulting distortions of consumption patterns tend to increase the dependency of recipients on continued food aid. When young babies are given dried milk, for example, their mothers cannot suddenly switch on their own milk again when the aid ceases.

However, aid in the wider sense, including soft loans channelled through UN institutions, has had more success (according to the World Bank), especially where the funds are used to finance specific projects and where the recipient country organises itself so as to make efficient use of the funds received.

FIGURE 8.1
Money Flows to LDCs from IMF and World Bank

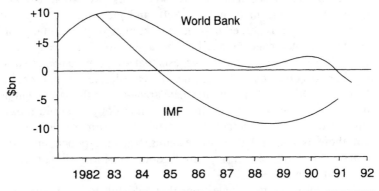

SOURCE   UNDP, *Human Development Report*, 1992.

Critics would say that institutional aid of this sort places too much faith in trickle-down economics, is overly concentrated on urban and industrial sectors, and that money should be directed to the poorest in society, developing the rural areas, increasing the spending power of the poor, and generating a demand for locally-produced goods. Figure 8.1 shows that even concessionary loans can cause a debt-servicing burden, and can actually result in net flows of money *out* of the LDCs.

In response to those who claim on the one hand that without aid many LDCs would be substantially worse off than they are today, or on the other hand that aid is in reality a barrier to progress, perhaps the most sensible conclusion to come to is that the amount of aid flowing from the MDCs to the LDCs for purely economic or commercial objectives has in fact been too small to have made much difference either way in all except the very poorest LDCs. The amount of aid directed at military and political purposes has probably had far greater impact on everyday lives, in those countries unfortunate enough to have played host to military advisers from the USA or the old USSR. However, the LDCs themselves show little desire to wean themselves away from aid, and generally still regard it as an important ingredient in their development.

How much aid?

In the late 1970s an international group of eminent economists and politicians formed an Independent Commission on International Development Issues, under the chairmanship of the former Chancellor of West Germany, Willy Brandt. In 1980 they published *North–South: A Programme for Survival*, otherwise known as the *Brandt Report*. This called for the amount of *official development assistance* (ODA) given each year to be increased to 0.7 per cent of the GNP of MDCs by 1985, and 1 per cent by the year 2000. The 0.7 per cent target, originally put forward by the United Nations, was reasserted at the Rio Summit in 1992. Very few MDCs are anywhere near this target: only Denmark, Norway, the Netherlands and Sweden have achieved it for any length of time. Moreover, since aid can be very ambiguously defined, everything from genuine grant aid to slightly concessional loans could be included. For this reason the OECD Development Assistance Committee (DAC) has tried to persuade members that the grant element of ODA should be at least 80 per cent.

Britain's aid budget has been falling for the last thirty years. Back in the early 1960s, it was over 0.5 per cent of GNP, but dropped below 0.4 per cent in 1982 and 0.3 per cent in 1990, despite a spirited fight to increase it by the aid minister Baroness Chalker from 1986 until 1997. Today, the aid budget is just under 2 billion pounds, and was projected to fall further by the outgoing Conservative government. About two-thirds is ODA spent directly in over 150 countries, and one-third is spent through the IMF/World Bank and the EU. Within the EU, aid is pulled in many directions. The Germans favour Eastern Europe, the French favour West Africa and Spain favours Latin America, all for historically understandable reasons. The Labour government elected in 1997 immediately upgraded and renamed its aid administration as the Department for International Development, made it independent of the Foreign Office and gave it a minister of Cabinet rank. It remains to be seen whether the percentage share of GNP will rise under Clare Short.

Looking at the overall financial relationship between MDCs and LDCs, loans, aid and investment form the flow from the rich to the poor countries. Profits, interest and repayment of earlier debts are the main ingredients of the flow from poor to rich countries. Cutting the aid budget can cause the disturbing result of a net flow from the poor to the rich. According to the *New Internationalist* magazine, this was as much as 4 billion pounds to Britain alone in 1990.

Government, Externalities and the Environment

9

What is the role of government in economic development? What effects can development have on the environment? Should governments intervene to attempt to control these effects?

An Appropriate Level of Government Intervention?

Economic thought evolves largely in the universities and finance ministries of the MDCs, and is transmitted to the governments of LDCs through multilateral agencies and the global banking system. Thus the level of government intervention considered appropriate in development varies over time according to the dominance of particular schools of economic thought and their political interpretation. In theory there are limiting cases: the *command economy* where all decision making is centralised and the entirely *free-market economy* where all resource allocation decisions are decentralised. These extremes have immense and unacceptable social costs: behind the 'point of a gun' policies used in China's Great Leap Forward and Stalin's early five-year plans lie human tragedies on a vast scale; and ultimate freedom in labour markets would imply acceptance of slavery.

In reality all economies are 'mixed' to some extent, in that there is no such thing as a purely planned economy, nor is there such a thing as a complete free-market economy with no government intervention; but even in the western democracies traditionally described as mixed economies there has been a fierce debate about the degree of planning and the extent to which prices should be freely determined.

Macroeconomic Policy in the Post-war World

From 1945 until the mid 1970s, MDC governments especially in Europe attempted, following Keynesian demand management ideas, to intervene in the market economy in order to 'stabilise' certain economic variables. They sought the simultaneous stabilisation of prices, trade balances, exchange rates, employment levels, and economic growth rates. Full employment was the first priority, because regulating the *income* available for the purchase of goods and services would promote the stability from which growth would spring. A substantial state sector was permissible as a stabilising influence. The main weapons of demand management were monetary policy (influencing the interest rates and the availability of credit) and budgetary or fiscal policy (adjusting government expenditure and revenue). At certain times and places, Keynesian policies had considerable success: following World War II, for instance, the United Kingdom experienced two decades of unemployment at rates of around 2 per cent, approximately one-tenth of rates in the early 1930s and one-fifth of rates in the 1980s.

However, Keynesian policies became difficult to implement when objectives conflicted. It often seemed, for instance, that there were 'trade-offs' between full employment, price stability and external viability, and that achieving one of these objectives worsened the others. Success in achieving full employment caused overheating which led to inflation and lost competitiveness. In some LDCs, for example in South America, the attempt to use demand management policies together with exogenous shocks and weak monetary policy could lead to levels of inflation in excess of 1000 per cent; if governments do not react effectively to problems of this sort then the welfare losses and social costs are tremendous, as the value of hard-earned savings are wiped out overnight, and a significant barrier to development is created as prudent foreign investors take care to avoid transactions in such an unstable currency. Brazil has been forced to change its currency four times in the last twenty years.

The devastating social effects of hyperinflation should not blind us to the equally bad, or even worse effects of mass unemployment. If human development is defined as a process of 'extending choice', then the opportunity to earn one's own wage, rather than to be dependent on charity or state hand-outs, is an important part of the empowerment of citizens. With global population levels projected to double within a couple of decades, the problem of unemployment can be described as a political and economic time bomb.

Macroeconomic Policy in Recent Times

The apparent failure of Keynesian policies opened the way for a less-interventionist phase from the early 1980s, associated with the adoption of monetarism by the Reagan and Thatcher governments. Monetarists would disagree with Keynesians on the precise methods of government intervention; they would also argue that there is no long-term trade-off between inflation and unemployment, but that stable prices are a necessary and sufficient condition to create jobs. Therefore, given a choice between short-run job creation and deflationary policies to reduce price increases, they would give a higher priority to anti-inflation measures than Keynesians might favour. In the first half of the 1980s the British government believed that setting a target for money supply would control inflation and bring price stability, but the social costs proved disastrous: the economy shrank by 2.2 per cent in 1980, nearly 30 per cent of industrial capacity was lost between 1979 and 1982, and unemployment grew from 1.1 million to over 3 million in the same three years.

Since monetarists see the main cause of inflation as being increases in the money supply, and since they also see governments, through their borrowing operations, as being the main cause of increases in the money supply, they naturally argue for less government involvement in the economy than would be advocated by Keynesians. A school of economic thought known as *supply-side economics* has taken this idea a stage further, and has provided support for the trend towards privatisation, anti-trade union legislation to free labour markets, and reductions in direct tax rates. These policies have been transmitted through the compulsory conditionality of multilateral aid programmes to many LDCs.

The fashion for reducing the role of government to uncover the profit-seeking instincts of the private sector has spread throughout the world in the 1990s. For example, there had been over 800 privatisations of substantial state assets in the world by 1995, most of them supervised by the British merchant banks who pioneered the sale of huge utilities such as British Telecom and British Gas in 1984.

A phrase often used by advocates of free market economics to justify the shrinking of the state sector is *trickle-down*. Less government activity means lower taxes, and a shift from progressive direct taxes such as income tax to indirect taxes such as sales taxes should doubly relieve the tax burden on the rich. Entrepreneurs, previously discouraged by high taxes, would now unleash their competitive instincts and create jobs and growth that would trickle down through the economy. There is little empirical evidence to support this. Growth rates in Britain and America have been lower in the 1980s than they were in the 1970s, and are lower still in the 1990s. Trickle-down has, however, resulted in the growth of inequality and a disenfranchised underclass in the MDCs. But the idea that deliberately fostering inequality can have economic benefits has an altogether different resonance in the LDCs. Oxfam recently published a report entitled *Growth with Equity* which shows that the countries which have been most successful in achieving development, typically South East Asian countries, have *more* equal income distribution than less successful economies in Latin America where inequality is greatest. Why should this be the case? Firstly, in an economy which is dominated by the demand of a rich elite, such as Brazil, high-priced branded imports and servants will be important. This will not lead to broad-fronted growth. Secondly, in an economy where redistribution through taxes is acceptable, there exists the possibility of investment in human capital through the education system and in infrastructure schemes to reduce the costs of economic activity to all. These are clear characteristics of the Asian Tiger economies, where much government spending goes towards increasing the *social wage* – the value received by all citizens as of right through education, healthcare, etc.

The latest orthodoxy in macroeconomic policy-making in the MDCs is concerned with controlling cyclical fluctuations. The main weapon used to slow down over-rapid growth or stimulate sluggish economies is interest rates. As has been shown in Chapter 8, raising interest rates as a matter of domestic monetary policy in MDCs has the side-effect of increasing debt-servicing costs of LDCs.

Types of Planning

Even though the centrally-planned economy of the Soviet type is rare and likely to become extinct except in history books, it remains useful to consider types of planning since elements of it exist in most economies.

Comprehensive planning, Soviet-style, involved using 'commands' emanating from government agencies to determine not only output, but the inputs which were used in production. The transformation of the Soviet Union from a backward agrarian country in 1917, to a military power strong enough to defeat Nazi Germany on the Eastern Front in World War II, to a space-exploring nuclear superpower – all within 50 years – indicates that comprehensive planning can achieve a great deal. However, the movement away from the comprehensiveness of planning in the 1990s indicates its many shortcomings, chief among which was the inability to satisfy consumer choice. Some LDCs, such as India, have attempted to use the techniques of comprehensive planning, including *input-output analysis* – a mathematical method for predicting the amount of raw materials, components and labour which will be required to meet the demand for a target output of final goods. However, when LDCs lack the staff or statistical techniques to produce accurate figures, input-output analysis is of little help to policy-makers. Even if they can predict the need for investment in certain productive sectors, they might not have enough control over commercial and financial markets to direct investment into these sectors. And even countries with well-developed systems for comprehensive planning find it difficult to predict and adjust to exogenous shocks, such as changes in fuel oil prices.

Formal planning, in contrast to comprehensive planning, makes far more use of markets. It involves the government putting forward a detailed national economic plan, arrived at in consultation with the private sector, and setting targets for economic indicators such as exports or investment. It usually involves a minimum of government intervention beyond achieving this consensus, and the government steers clear of attempting to actually implement the plan, other than by using it to convince foreign investors and UN agencies that the country is working towards rational objectives. This approach was fashionable in Western Europe in the 1960s.

Indicative planning involves the government making predictions of what it expects to happen in the private economy, and will usually include deliberate action by the state, including taxes and subsidies, investment incentives, or direct investment by the government in infrastructure projects to attempt to ensure that the plan is implemented and its targets met. What is crucially important is that the private sector should have confidence in government predictions, and invest accordingly. In France, where indicative planning has been used extensively, this meant making investment decisions that were binding for periods longer than the time between elections, making projects safe from party politics.

All MDCs and most LDCs carry out at least some form of planning; what differs is the degree of intervention, and also the techniques used to appraise investment decisions. In response to an increased awareness of externalities, many countries are taking more interest in the use of techniques such as *cost-benefit analysis*, which attempts to quantify those aspects of planning which do not always show up on a balance sheet, and so gives decision-makers more information upon which to base their policies.

Public Goods, Merit Goods and Natural Monopolies

Even in free market economies, state intervention is often found in the provision of *public goods*. These are best provided by the state because they are:

- *non-excludable* (individuals cannot be stopped from consuming them);
- *non-diminishable* (one person's use does not deprive another).

Examples are national defence, law and order, and public health measures (such as clean air and the eradication of infectious diseases). Provision at all means provision for all, and it is unlikely that their provision could be achieved by any supplier other than the state, which has access through taxes to the funds necessary to provide them. Because of non-excludability and non-diminishablilty, no private supplier would offer a public good because it would be unable to exclude free riders. LDCs, with their narrow tax base, find the provision of public goods expensive but very necessary.

Governments also find it necessary to intervene to provide goods and services which do not respond very well to price signals. These goods and services would be underconsumed at market price, because they are expensive but not wanted at all times. They are known as are *merit goods*, and are high in positive externalities: that is they benefit both the user and non-user. Education and hospital treatment are examples. The relatively high levels of spending on education in the Asian Tiger economies produces a literate and numerate workforce with consequent benefits in labour productivity. Conversely, some goods are *demerit goods*, and their use harms the non-user: the effects of passive smoking on non-users of tobacco is an example.

TABLE 9.1
Effects of Externalities

Main Features	Type of Goods		
	Public goods	*Merit goods*	*Private goods*
Diminishability	Non-Diminishable	Diminishable	Diminishable
Excludability	Non-Excludable	Excludable (but their full benefits are not felt by those who are included)	Excludable
Benefits	Communal (mainly positive externalities)	Individual and communal (strong positive externalities)	Individual (mainly internalities)
Provider	*Usually* the government	Government and/ or private enterprise	*Usually* private enterprise
Financed by	*Usually* taxation (the 'ability to pay' principle)	Taxes and/or prices	*Usually* through the price system (the 'beneficial' principle)
Examples	National defence; law and order; street lights; light houses	Health; Education; Roads	Corn Flakes; Clothes; TV sets; etc.

Natural monopolies exist where services are more efficiently provided by one supplier than by many. In the case of piped water, sewerage services, and the national grid for electricity distribution, where a huge expensive infrastructure is necessary, the existence of competing suppliers would be a waste of resources involving unnecessary duplication. Economies of scale enjoyed by the single supplier far outweigh any efficiency gains from competition. To prevent the abuse of monopoly power, and to ensure that any producer surplus is returned to the community, it is only 'natural' that the enterprise should be run from the centre, and therefore owned by the state.

Externalities, the Environment and Government Intervention

The strongest case for government intervention in the economy arises from *market failure*. Market failure occurs for three reasons widely known to economics students: the resource misallocation that stems from any departure from perfect competition, slowness of markets to react to disequilibrium, and externalities. As economic development takes place there is bound to be an increase in both the production and consumption of goods and services. Production and consumption both involve the creation of costs and benefits, and these costs and benefits can be internal or private (experienced only by the individual producer or consumer), or they can be external or public (side-effects experienced not only by the producer or consumer, but also by the community at large). So the full costs to society (social costs) of any act of production or consumption will consist of both the private costs and the public side-effects, which could be positive or negative. Some examples will illustrate this rather complicated set of propositions.

- The destruction of thousands of hectares of rain forest at Rondonia in Brazil for open-cast tin mining from 1987 is an example of a *negative production externality*. The private costs of extracting the tin ore were met by the mining company, but the cost to society in lost biodiversity and habitat was not paid because no-one has ownership rights over such abstract ideas. These costs to society can only be recovered through governments controlling the mining companies and forcing them to pay for reafforestation if such measures are feasible. Allowing firms to escape payment of total social costs leads them to overproduce.
- The building of access roads for trucks to remote tea plantations in Kenya in the 1960s had a *positive production externality*. Children from remote communities were able to reach schools and

receive education, raising literacy levels and improving human capital. This benefit to society was paid for by the road builders, who might have been encouraged to build more roads by government or a foreign aid donor. The best aid schemes have high positive externalities.

- The polluted atmosphere from car and motorcycle exhaust in Mexico City is an example of a *negative consumption externality*. The cost to the consumer of using his car does not take full account of the air pollution, once again because of the lack of ownership rights to the atmosphere. Government might discourage private car use through taxation or licences, or even subsidise the use of public transport because it has *positive consumption externalities*: greater use of buses and trains reduces accidents, pollution and congestion.

This gives us one reason why governments need to intervene in the economy, because if internal and external costs and benefits can be estimated, then economic welfare can be increased if a negative externality is taxed, and a positive one is subsidised. These actions 'internalise' the externalities, and so force the producer or consumer to consider the full social costs (or benefits) of their actions. Thus a firm polluting a river, for example, and relying on the taxpayer to pay for its dirty work, could be forced by taxation to reflect the pollution costs in higher prices and/or lower profits. The 'polluter pays' idea is one which today receives a great deal of support (in principle at least) from economists and politicians alike.

Much of the debate about the environment has originated in the MDCs where ownership rights are better defined and people are more prone to litigation. Also the MDCs are rich enough to care about the environment in ways that mystify some LDCs. The Brazilian interior minister recently responded sharply to European criticism of damage to rain forests by pointing out that Europe felled most of its forest in earlier centuries and got rich. Was Brazil not allowed to do the same? China's declared intention to develop by exploiting its coal reserves causes similar dismay in the MDCs. Resource conservation is seen in some LDCs as a luxury, and it is certainly true that some environmental damage is a consequence of poverty rather than growth. People in absolute poverty are unable to conserve water or wood in aquifers or forests.

Sustainable Development

In 1987 the UN World Commission on Environment and Development (the *Brundtland Commission*) defined sustainable development as development that meets the needs of the present without compromising the ability of future generations to meet their own needs. This is interpreted by Ian Hodge in his sister volume to this book, *Environmental Economics*, in the following terms: if the environment is viewed as a stock of natural capital, nothing should be done which affects the total value passed on over successive generations. For example, forests and fisheries should be exploited at or below their rates of renewal, waste should be dumped at rates at or below what the environment can absorb and process, and exploitation of non-renewable resources such as oil should not exceed the rate at which renewable resources are developed or conservation and changes in technology reduce the demand for energy. Many difficulties arise from the measurement of these variables, and the data disagreements which seem so common among environmental scientists.

Centralisation and Decentralisation

In considering the 'proper' degree of government intervention the above points are helpful in discussing the amount of centralisation (nationalisation) or decentralisation (privatisation) which is appropriate. The distribution and sale of foodstuffs, for example, is best done in a decentralised way; shopkeepers are far better than government officials at detecting the wants and tastes of consumers. In a country like the UK, where the efficiency of retailing has been developed to a fine degree, no economist in their right minds would advocate the nationalisation of the retail chains such as Sainsbury or Tesco. In the case of telecommunications, where satellite and radio links mean that new technology will liberate suppliers from the heavy infrastructure of copper wires, a once natural monopoly will probably evolve into a very competitive market, where decentralised suppliers will be able to respond to consumer wants very quickly indeed: privatisation will therefore create welfare gains.

The privatisation of natural monopolies such as water, sewerage and electricity has been done in the UK, and debate continues over whether this was a wise move. Before this debate is finally settled, the

MDCs are exporting the idea to the LDCs, and to the new market economies of Eastern Europe, as if the welfare gains of privatisation were a proven fact. If economic development is to improve the human condition in the widest possible sense, then there is surely a central role for government in providing the basic utilities. In the case of merit goods, not even the most enthusiastic free-marketeer would advocate that LDCs should privatise elementary education, as the positive externalities of improved basic literacy are so obviously high; where there is room for some debate about the role of market prices is with merit goods such as higher education, where the private benefits of qualifications at this level, through improved job prospects, perhaps warrant some degree of contribution from the user. Even here, however, if the qualifications are to be relevant to the national programmes for development, then some central coordination and hence government planning will always be necessary.

Areas of Concern

Pollution, disease and war are barriers to human development which markets are almost powerless to prevent. Over the last 20 years, the world has undergone dramatic changes in the pressures that human consumption and production has put on its natural resources. There are now 428 nuclear reactors in 31 countries. There have been two serious accidents, at Three Mile Island, USA, in 1979, and Chernobyl, Ukraine, in 1986. Each year, over 23 billion tons of carbon dioxide are released into the atmosphere, 50 per cent more than in 1973. The burning of forests (170 000 square kilometres per year), and the increased use of motor vehicles will add more. The world has over 600 million motor vehicles, most of which are in the MDCs. The LDCs represent from one point of view a huge untapped market for the motor industry; from another point of view the potential for a rapid acceleration in global warming and other problems. Why should the LDCs show restraint in burning fossil fuels as part of their transport policy when the MDCs set no such example? Whereas 20 years ago no-one knew to what extent chlorine was destroying the ozone layer, today we know that the concentration has been doubling every fifteen years or so, enough to open a hole in the layer above the Antartic each spring. Natural species are disappearing. With 90 million tonnes of fish being caught each year (nearly twice as much as twenty years ago) fish stocks are at a risk of total collapse. Many species of animal are becoming extinct, on a scale which last occurred during the Ice Age. As we have seen, diseases such as Aids and Cholera affect all countries, but strike disproportionately in the LDCs.

In 1996 global arms sales reached $31.8 billion out of which $19.3 billion went to LDCs. The biggest LDC customers were India ($2.5 billion), Saudi Arabia ($1.9 billion), South Korea ($1.2 billion), and Indonesia ($1 billion). War refugees are estimated to number 28 million. At the same time, there are increasing numbers of economic refugees, crossing national borders to seek work, often illegally, and thus being exposed to exploitation and dangerous working conditions.

Such problems are not problems for the LDCs alone. It is no longer possible for the inhabitants of MDCs to regard distant problems in far off lands as having 'nothing to do with us', although the insensitivity of officials who should know better sometimes defies belief. In February 1992 the chief economist of the World Bank was reported as having written a secret memorandum which suggested that rich nations could export their hazardous waste products to the poor. These reports reinforced the views of those who believe that the World Bank takes a cynical view of sustainable development and regards the environment as taking a lower priority than the generation of wealth. They also indicate a lack of awareness of the economic externalities involved in such matters as greenhouse gases, pollution of international waters, protecting the ozone layer, and preserving biodiversity.

In the final analysis, problems like the disposal of waste products cannot be exported; any attempt by the MDCs to put them out of sight and out of mind will return to haunt them.

All the problems mentioned in this chapter affect rich and poor alike; but their impact on the LDCs is particularly severe. They are problems which do not stop at national boundaries. They are problems where externalities swamp the internalities. They will not be solved by markets; they will not even be solved by national governments. The only hope of making any progress with any of them is through international action.

Some Conclusions

For over twenty years UNCTAD has been calling for a 'New International Economic Order', which involves a package of measures aimed at addressing some of the problems which LDCs complain about in their trading relations with MDCs. These include suggested ways of raising commodity prices through international agreements, and the creation of new institutions, such as a Development Security Council to replace GATT. No sooner had these relatively modest proposals failed to make any progress, when the 'superpowers' among the MDCs announced a 'New World Order' which would right wrongs, firstly in the Gulf, and then elsewhere. No sooner had the Gulf War failed to achieve any meaningful rights for Kurds or Marsh Arabs, when Western leaders turned their attention to the apparently insoluble problems of the Balkan states. No sooner had...we had better stop before we get too dismal. Is the future course of international relations destined to be a breeding ground for pessimists, or are there some rays of hope? Is the 'science' of economics powerful enough to offer any meaningful policies for tackling the awesome problems of the LDCs? If, as one famous politician has claimed, there is 'no such thing as society, only individuals' why should wealthier individuals and countries be concerned about the problems of LDCs?

There is one simple answer, and this answer goes to the very heart of economics. It is called 'opportunity cost'. The notion of opportunity cost draws our attention to the fact that this planet's resources are finite. We are all faced with scarcity and we all have to make choices. By considering opportunity costs we can analyse what would have happened if we had followed an alternative course of action to the one we actually chose. In an interdependent world, as John Donne noted a long time ago, there is no need to ask for whom the bell tolls; we will find that there is only one thing more costly than choosing to address development issues, and that is choosing not to address them.

One thing which Western world leaders have not provided is world leadership. If the ineffectual nature of the Rio Earth Summit is not to be repeated, then there are two main issues to be addressed.

Firstly, MDCs need new economic priorities and strategies. Growth based, for example, on the export of the output of military-related industries is, in the long run, unsustainable growth. As the Gulf War demonstrated, such exports have a nasty habit of hitting back at their country of origin. MDCs need a new direction for their own development; one based on the quality of life. We must face the fact that the ecology of this planet might eventually have to be shared among more than 10 billion people.

Secondly, the MDCs must realise that their own survival is threatened by development in the LDCs and the former Soviet bloc, if it is the type of development that damages the environment's ecosystems. New patterns of trade, investment and aid are needed to support development which is on a human scale, and which provides infrastructure whose purpose is to support local people rather than displace them.

There are grounds for optimism in the growing awareness that many problems are international: pollution and global warming, for example. Everyone is contributing to the gases and wastes which foul up our air and sea. There is growing awareness of the fact that the world's natural systems are inter-linked; that the rain forests of Brazil help purify the air over Europe; that the power stations of Britain help contaminate the air over Scandinavia with acid rain. Let us also hope that increased awareness of the evils of international trade in landmines will spill over into a general distaste for the products of military-dependent industries.

From the wider perspective of human development, encompassing concerns for the quality of life, there are also grounds for optimism in the beginnings of social awareness we see in the arrangements between some of the trading blocs. The Social Chapter of the EU's Treaty of Maastricht, for instance, sets down minimum provisions for basic working conditions and working hours. Human development in the long run surely depends on the MDCs setting minimum standards towards which the citizens of the LDCs can aspire, rather than attempting the impossible by trying to compete with the unlimited capacity of the LDCs to provide multi-national enterprises with sweated labour.

On a more disappointing note, the attitude of the world's largest polluter, the United States, at the environmental conference in Kyoto, Japan in 1997 seriously undermined international attempts to reduce the emissions (mainly from the products of the motor car industry) which threaten to increase global warming, and cast doubt over inter-governmental ability to resist the demands for continued economic growth (as opposed to development) which emanate from both domestic politics and multinational global corporatism.

Another cause for serious concern, both for economic development and the environment, is the way in which the Tiger Economies of East Asia went into free-fall during the summer of 1997, with the Thailand Baht falling by 40 per cent of its value, South Korea having to be bailed out by the IMF, major banks and manufacturers throughout the region collapsing, and jungle fires lit by forestry concerns anxious to use the land to earn liquidity causing spectacular smoke pollution. The repercussions have still to be fully felt in the MDCs; the future of those parts of the Japanese banking sector which have financed the rise of the Tigers is precarious; while Western economies which have encouraged inward investment from the region are vulnerable to any recessionary effects.

Another cause for serious concern is the under-publicised Multilateral Agreement on Investment (MAI) which threatens to undermine local control of property and labour markets, and could swing the balance of power towards multinationals and against state governments (especially of LDCs), by outlawing many measures which have been designed to improve the quality of life.

Finally, a prediction. Development economics will increasingly focus on the idea of *sustainable* development. The full cost of consuming resources and creating externalities will have to be built into prices. Markets and governments will have to work in harmony to achieve this; neither can achieve it in isolation. The global consumer economy will need to be examined critically, and intergovernmental action will be needed to ensure that the priorities of the MNEs correspond with the best interests of the majority of world citizens. Most difficult of all: we will all have to try to educate ourselves to consume only what we can replace.

Index

Key: Ch = chapter;   ff = and following pages
(Individually named cities/countries/regions are indexed where they are mentioned in the text; others which are mentioned in charts and tables are generally not indexed.)